200 jams & preserves

D0544571

80003275526

Quince cheese

Apple, apricot & elderflower butter

St Clement's curd

hamlyn | all colour cookbook

200 jams & preserves

Sara Lewis

Strawberry jam

Minted blackberry & apple jelly

Peach Melba conserve

An Hachette UK Company
www.hachette.co.uk

First published in Great Britain in 2012 by Hamlyn
a division of Octopus Publishing Group Ltd
Endeavour House, 189 Shaftesbury Avenue
London WC2H 8JY
www.octopusbooks.co.uk

All rights reserved. No part of this book may be reproduced
or utilized in any form or by any means, electronic or
mechanical, including photocopying, recording or by any
information storage or retrieval system, without the prior
written permission of the publisher.

ISBN: 978-0-600-62412-7

A CIP catalogue record for this book is available
from the British Library

Printed and bound in China

1 2 3 4 5 6 7 8 9 10

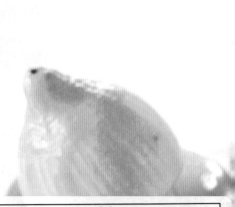

Both metric and imperial measurements have
been given in all recipes. Use one set of
measurements only, and not a mixture of both.

Standard level spoon measurements are used in all recipes
1 tablespoon = 15 ml spoon
1 teaspoon = 5 ml spoon

Fresh herbs should be used unless otherwise stated.
Medium eggs should be used unless otherwise stated.
Freshly ground black pepper should be used
unless otherwise stated.

This book includes dishes made with nuts and nut
derivatives. It is advisable for those with known allergic
reactions to nuts and nut derivatives or those who may be
potentially vulnerable to these allergies, such as pregnant
and nursing mothers, invalids, the elderly, babies and
children, to avoid dishes made with these. It is prudent
to check the labels of all pre-prepared ingredients for the
possible inclusion of nut derivatives.

The Department of Health advises that eggs should not be
consumed raw. This book contains some dishes made with
raw or lightly cooked eggs. It is prudent for more vulnerable
people such as pregnant and nursing mothers, invalids, the
elderly, babies and young children to avoid uncooked or
lightly cooked dishes made with eggs.

Northamptonshire Libraries & Information Service KR		
Askews & Holts	2012	

contents

introduction

introduction

Making homemade preserves is going through a revival as the trend for local produce grows. Nothing is more rewarding than picking your own fruit and gathering enough strawberries to make a batch of jam, or growing your own fruit and veg to make chutneys and pickles.

If you are new to making preserves, read through the introduction before you begin. Preserves are not difficult to make, but it is important to maintain the balance of fruit to sugar when making jams, jellies or marmalade, or sugar to vinegar when making chutney. A chutney or a fruit curd is perhaps the best place to start; there are no tests for setting required – just keep cooking and stirring until thick. They make great gifts, especially if packaged with ribbons or raffia and decorative labels.

Preparing jams, jellies and marmalades requires a little more attention, but the finished results are worth the care. Over the next few pages you will find all the information you need with helpful step-by-step pictures and tips. Making preserves is relaxing and not something to be rushed. Chopping and shredding can be wonderfully calming, while the smell of the fruits gently simmering soon permeates the house with a wonderful aroma.

Who's who

If you are new to making jams and chutneys, you may be a little confused by the terms. Here is a brief explanation of some of them.

Chutneys – these are sweet and sour and made with vinegar, sugar, spices and chopped fresh fruits, dried fruits, usually with a base of chopped onions plus tomatoes or cooking apples. All the ingredients are added to the preserving pan at once, then cooked 'low and slow' until thick. Serve with cheese, cold meats or sausages, or add to sandwiches.

Conserves – similar to a jam but with a slightly softer set, these have a high proportion of large or whole pieces of fruit. Boil with sugar until setting point is reached. Serve spread on bread or toast, or spoon over ice cream.

Jams – most often made with crushed or diced fruits. Boil with sugar until setting point is reached. Firmer than a conserve but not as set as a jelly.

Jellies – a crystal-clear preserve, best made with fruits that have pips or seeds, or are fiddly to prepare, as the fruit needs just

chopping with no need to peel or core first. Cook gently just covered with water until soft, then strain through a jelly bag. Measure sugar and add 500 g (1 lb) for every 600 ml (1 pint) of strained liquid. Boil until setting point is reached. Serve in the same way as a jam. Savoury jellies can be made with a mix of water and vinegar, boiled with sugar and flavoured with herbs, spices or peppercorns. Delicious served with roast meats, game, grilled fish or cold ham.

Fruit butters – a kind of jam made with poached fruit that is puréed and sieved. For every 500 g (1 lb) purée add between 250 g (8 oz) and 375 g (12 oz) sugar, then cook gently until reduced almost by half and the mixture is thick and glossy. Rather like a chutney, these don't need to be boiled to reach setting point. Popular with children who dislike 'bits'.

Fruit cheeses – quince cheese or membrillo is perhaps the most popular. Again made with a fruit purée but with a higher ratio of sugar at 375 g (12 oz) to 500 g (1 lb) sugar to every 500 g (1 lb) purée. Like fruit butter, the mixture is cooked gently until reduced and very thick. As there is more sugar, this sets firmly and is best spooned into oiled wide-necked jars. Serve sliced as part of a cheese course.

Fruit curds – the most popular is perhaps lemon curd where fruit juice and grated fruit rind is mixed with sugar, butter and beaten eggs and cooked in a bain-marie or a bowl set over a saucepan of gently simmering water until thick. Fruit curds can also be made with puréed fruits, but this method is most suited to sharper, more acidic fruits, such as apples, gooseberries or soft fruits mixed with a citrus fruit. As they contain eggs and butter, fruit curds must be stored in the refrigerator and consumed within a few weeks.

Marmalades – traditionally made with whole Seville oranges that are cooked until soft, then finely cut into strips and boiled with sugar until setting point is reached. As the availability of Seville oranges is so short, generally only between February and March, an alternative is to use a variety of oranges and mix with lemons and limes.

Mincemeat – a Christmas preserve made with boozy soaked dried fruits, grated apple, sugar and spices and served in pastry cases.

Pickles – these can be made with vegetables, first soaked in a dry salt mix or brine to draw out the juices, then rinsed and packed while raw or blanched for a few minutes with flavoured vinegar or a thickened spiced vinegar. Whole apricots or plums or halved peaches can also be pickled in a sweetened vinegar mix. Serve with salads, cold meats, cheese or smoked fish.

Relishes – these can be cooked or uncooked and tend to be hotter and more intense than a chutney. Serve with curries, cold meats or barbecued foods. Uncooked relishes must be stored in the refrigerator and served within a day or two of making.

equipment

Must haves

Preserving pan – most have sloping sides with, ideally, a spout to help you pour the jam from the pan, plus either two small handles or one large arched handle that can be locked upright or folded flat when not in use and a smaller second handle, enabling you to lift the pan safely on and off the cooker, and to tip to empty. They can vary in size but are generally around 30 cm (12 inches) across the top and about 18 cm (7 inches) deep, so that there is room for evaporation and little chance that the jam will boil over. Never fill more than half full.

Try to buy the best quality that you can. Heavy-based aluminium pans are the most durable and widely available, while stainless steel ones are the most expensive. If possible, choose a pan with a lid so that you can gently simmer fruits, but if not improvise with a large piece of foil or a baking sheet.

If you are not sure how much jam you may make in the future, buy second-hand.

Skimming spoon – a large flat spoon with small perforations used to remove scum easily from the surface of the boiling jam.

Sugar thermometer – add this large metal thermometer to the preserving pan while the jam heats up. Ideally, choose one with a clip to hold it in place over the side of the pan without sliding into the jam. Never plunge the thermometer into boiling jam; always bring the temperature up gradually. For jam, the thermometer should read 105°C (221°F).

Jam funnel – this has a top the size of a small plate or saucer with a wide-necked spout that

is about 3.5 cm (1 ½ inches) long so that it sits easily over a jar. Invaluable for ladling or pouring jam into jars to minimize spills.

Jelly bag – this cone-shaped bag can be made with flannel, felt, linen or fine nylon mesh. It has strings or long loops at the top so that the bag can be suspended from an upturned stool over a large bowl (make sure to rinse the bowl and bag with boiling water before use) or from a specially designed frame. It is great for making jellies: spoon in the cooked fruit and water and allow to drip for 3–4 hours, or overnight. Resist the urge to squeeze the bag or the juice will be cloudy. The closer the mesh or weave of the fabric the clearer the juice. If you are new to preserving, or not sure how often you will use a jelly bag, improvise with a double-thickness layer of muslin that has been soaked in boiling water, then draped into a large nylon sieve set over a bowl. After use, empty the jelly bag and wash well in hot water, but don't use detergent. Dry thoroughly before storing in a plastic bag.

Muslin and string – buy muslin from your local fabric shop. Cut off as much as you need and soak in boiling water for 5 minutes to sterilize before use. Drain and leave until cool enough to handle. Use to wrap whole spices, or citrus fruit pips and pith, and tie with string before adding to the pan. Squeeze well at the end of cooking and discard the contents; wash and recycle the muslin, depending on the size.

Items that you are sure to have

Scales – accuracy is important to ensure a good set.

Roasting tin – useful to warm sugar before adding to fruit and to hold jam jars as they sterilize in the oven.

Wooden spoons and ladle – choose a wooden spoon with a long handle. A ladle is essential when potting jam.

Lemon squeezer – for squeezing juice from citrus fruits.

Fine sieve – choose a nylon or stainless-steel sieve so there is no chance that the fruit or vinegar will react with the sieve.

Vegetable peeler – to pare the fruit rind thinly with the minimum amount of pith.

Chopping board and knives – choose a large wooden chopping board. You'll also need a small vegetable knife for removing pith and membrane from oranges or coring apples, plus a large knife for finely shredding pared citrus rind or dicing fruit and vegetables.

Choosing fruit

Choose fruit that is ripe and fresh for the maximum flavour and pectin. Nearly any kind of fruit can be used in jams, jellies or conserves. Rinse hedgerow and supermarket fruits before use.

Fruits vary in the amount of pectin that they contain. Pectin is the gel-like substance essential to set jam and is found in varying amounts in the seeds, pips, cores and skins of fruits. When fruits are crushed and warmed, the pectin is released and mixes with the natural fruit acids to produce a jelly-like set. Fruits with lower amounts of pectin can be mixed with fruits with higher levels or with fresh lemon juice, or juice from redcurrants or gooseberries. Commercially prepared tartaric or citric acid is available in powdered form from chemists and can be mixed to a paste, 1 teaspoon powder to 1 tablespoon cold water, or buy liquid pectin from the supermarket and follow the instructions on the bottle.

TIP: The pectin in fruit makes the jam set, but it is the sugar that acts as the preservative.

making jams, jellies & marmalades
Step-by-step guide

  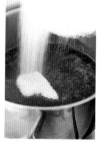

1 First cook the fruit with a little water over a gentle heat until just softened. Depending on the amount of water or firmness of the fruit, cook either covered or uncovered as specified in the recipe. Stir frequently to release the pectin and prevent the fruit from sticking.

2 Depending on the pectin content of the fruit, add lemon juice, citric acid or tartaric acid to boost the pectin levels.

3 Add warmed sugar and stir gently, still over low heat, with a wooden spoon until the sugar has completely dissolved.

PECTIN LEVELS

HIGH	cooking apples or sour green dessert apples, crab apples, cranberries, black, red and white currants, damsons, under-ripe gooseberries, grapefruit, grapes, japonicas, lemons, limes, loganberries, oranges, firm plums, quinces, rowanberries.
MEDIUM	dessert apples, fresh apricots, early blackberries, morello or may duke cherries, greengages, loganberries, mulberries, ripe plums, under-ripe raspberries, sloes.
LOW	sweet cherries, elderberries, medlars, melons, peaches, pears, pineapples, rhubarb, strawberries, vegetable marrows.

4 Increase the heat and boil the jam until setting point is reached, stirring very occasionally to prevent the fruit from sticking. The pan should be no more than half full so that there is plenty of room for the jam to boil without fear of it boiling over.

5 Skim the jam, if needed, with a skimming spoon, or stir in 15–25 g (½–1 oz) or 1–2 tablespoons butter to disperse the scum on the top. Ladle the jam, or pour it from a small heatproof jug, into warmed jars through a jam funnel.

Which sugar?

For most recipes, granulated sugar is a good choice, being reasonably priced and readily available. It dissolves easily and produces only minimal scum. Alternatively, you may prefer to use preserving sugar; this has slightly larger crystals, dissolves more quickly and produces minimal scum, but is more expensive. For fruit jams with low pectin levels, preserving sugar with added pectin and citric acid is a foolproof way to quickly bring a jam to setting point, and is most popular when making strawberry jam. For jams and marmalades with strong flavours, golden granulated or a mix of granulated and soft light muscovado or honey add extra flavour and depth for a darker finish.

Testing for setting

There are three main ways to check the setting point, but generally you will be able to tell if it is almost there as the jam will begin to lose height as it boils in the pan,

will make more noise and large bubbles will begin to form on the surface. It is important to watch the jam closely, but it usually takes 10–20 minutes to come to setting point. When you think it is ready, remove from the heat use one of the following tests:

Flake test – Gently stir, then lift the spoon out of the pan and hold so that it is vertical. If the jam forms a large blob or flake that very slowly drops from the spoon, it is ready. If it runs off in a thin stream, it isn't ready, so heat again and retry after a few minutes.

Saucer test – Place two or three saucers in the refrigerator before you begin jam making, so that they get very cold – or add a couple to the freezer if you forget when you begin dissolving the sugar. Remove from the heat when you think the jam is nearly ready, drop 2 teaspoons of the hot jam on to the cold plate, allow to cool for a minute or two, then run your index finger through the jam. If the top wrinkles and a path remains briefly, it is ready.

Thermometer test – Perhaps the most fail-safe method. Place a sugar thermometer in the jam when adding the sugar and allow to gradually come up to temperature. For a good set you need 105°C (221°F). Stir the jam before testing the temperature, as it can be hotter in the centre, or unclip and move the thermometer through the jam if preferred.

TIP: Getting the temperature right is crucial; just as a jam can be spoilt by being too runny,

overcooking can spoil the colour and flavour giving a much darker colour and very firm consistency. Begin testing after 10 minutes and then at 2–3-minute intervals.

What can go wrong?
Fruit floats to the surface
With conserves or jams that have a mixture of whole and mashed fruits, or chunky marmalade, it is important to leave the preserve to cool for 10–20 minutes until it just begins to wrinkle on the surface and starts to set. As the syrup will be thicker, the fruit will be held in suspension and be less likely to rise in the jar. Ladle into the warm jars, cover and seal.

Jam is very runny when potted
If you are new to jam-making, it can be difficult to tell if a set is correct, and you may pot jam before it is quite ready. If still soft the next day, simply pour the jam back into a pan and boil again. Use several different ways to test the set; first the flake test, with the thermometer to see if the jam is nearly ready, then back up with the saucer test.

Jam is very dark and set
Getting setting point absolutely right can be difficult and it is tempting to overcook. The longer the jam cooks the darker it will become and the more liquid will be driven off through evaporation, giving a much firmer set. As a rough guide, the finished jam should make 1½–2 times the amount of sugar used. When making marmalade, rather than using all brown sugar a mix of light muscovado and granulated sugar gives the best results.

Jelly looks cloudy
It is important to cook the fruit over a low heat until softened; don't try to speed up the process by turning up the heat. Likewise, after the cooked fruit and juice is spooned into the jelly bag, don't squeeze the bag as you will lose clarity in the finished jelly. Allow a minimum of 3–4 hours, preferably overnight, to drip through the bag.

Sugar has crystallized in the jar
When adding sugar, always heat gently, stirring occasionally, before bringing to a rolling boil and a set, or this can cause crystallization and the jam may taste a little crunchy. Alternatively, there could be too much sugar and the preserve was overboiled.

Jam tastes a little like wine
The fruit has fermented. This could be caused by insufficient cooking before the sugar was added, or insufficient sugar added.

Alternatively, the fruit was over-ripe when used. If you catch this in the early stages, transfer any unopened jars to the refrigerator or freezer to stop further fermentation. If freezing, transfer the contents of the glass jars to plastic containers with lids, leaving a headspace of 1 cm (½ inch) as the jam expands during freezing. Jam requires 60 per cent sugar if it is to keep well.

Surface of jam has a layer of mould

The seal on the jar is critical. Jam, jelly or marmalade should be potted when very hot; if using a screw-top lid fill right to the top, screw the lid on tightly, then leave to cool. As the jam cools and contracts slightly, an airtight seal will occur. If using a waxed disc and cellophane tops, the jam needn't be to the very top of the jar; fill to just a little below the rim, then top with a waxed disc, waxed side downwards, then a cellophane top securely fastened with an elastic band.

Jam can be left until cold, then covered with a waxed disc and cellophane top, but it is important that the jam is loosely covered with a lid or teacloth as it cools. If potting when cold, be very careful that the jam is carefully spooned into the jars and any air pockets dispersed with a small knife or skewer. Don't cover the jars when lukewarm, as condensation can collect and these damp conditions are perfect for mould, especially if the jars are then stored in a warm, steamy room. Once opened, store in the refrigerator.

finishing touches

Choosing jars

What better way to recycle than to reuse empty jam jars? Discard any with cracks or chips. Soak them and their lids in a bowl of warm soapy water to remove any odours, especially if reusing jars that have contained vinegar, then scrub jars well inside and out, taking care to clean inside the top of the lids.

For preserves made with larger fruits, such as pickled peaches or plums, you may prefer to pack the fruit into larger wide-necked springclip jars. These are available in a range of sizes but must be used with the rubber ring to ensure a good seal. Replacement rings can be bought if older rings show signs of wear.

If you have the older-style Kilner jars with gold rings and glass lids, or Fowler Lee jars with black metal clips, check them carefully and if the inside coating on the metal rings is scratched, don't use as the acid from the fruit will react and spoil the flavour.

If you plan to make preserves on a larger scale, it may be easier to buy jars online.

TIP: Sterilize all jars and screw-top lids after washing and just before filling. Rinse well with hot water to remove any soapy residues, drain and then stand them in a roasting tin. Warm in a preheated oven set to 160°C (325°F), Gas Mark 3, for 10 minutes. Alternatively, wash in a dishwasher and use while still warm, but make sure they are perfectly dry before filling.

For preserves that contain vinegar, choose a plastic-lined screw-top 63 mm (2.5 inches) thick metal lid. A plastic lining is essential so that the vinegar doesn't react with the metal lid to spoil the flavour of the preserve.

TIP: Screw-top lids can also be used on jams, jellies and marmalades. Fill the jar to the very top, screw on the lid and leave to cool. As the preserve cools and shrinks, a vacuum will occur producing an airtight seal. Don't be tempted to use both a waxed disc and screw-top lid as you may find that the waxed disc prevents the lid from making a tight seal.

Storage

Most preserves can be stored for 6 months or longer if kept in a cool, dark place. Choose a cupboard in the kitchen away from heat or light. If it is too warm the jam will shrink, too much light and the colour will fade, and any damp will make the preserve mouldy.

Chutneys taste even better if left for 2–3 weeks before use so that the flavours mellow.

Jams with reduced sugar can only be stored for a few weeks at room temperature and are best made in small quantities. If you have room in your refrigerator, you may prefer to keep them here to reduce any risk of moulds forming.

Fruit curds made with butter and eggs must be kept in the refrigerator and ideally eaten within 2–3 weeks if unopened, or within a few days if the seal is broken. Once any jar of preserve is opened, store in the refrigerator.

Covering

Traditionally, jams, jellies, mincemeat and marmalades are covered with waxed discs and cellophane tops attached with small elastic bands. These are inexpensive and easy to obtain in packs. The thin circle of waxed paper should be lightly pressed on to the surface of the preserve with the waxed side downwards, then the cellophane circle is pressed over the top of the jar and secured with an elastic band. The heat from the preserve causes the cellophane to make a tight seal.

jams &
conserves

strawberry jam

Makes **5–6 jars**
Preparation time **10 minutes**
Cooking time **20–30 minutes**

1.5 kg (3 lb) **strawberries**,
    hulled, halved or quartered
    depending on size
3 tablespoons freshly
    squeezed **lemon juice**
    (about 1½ lemons)
1.5 kg (3 lb) **jam sugar
    with pectin**
15 g (½ oz) **butter** (optional)

Add half the strawberries to a preserving pan and crush them roughly with a potato masher. Add the remaining strawberries and the lemon juice and heat gently for 15 minutes, until the fruit has softened.

Pour the sugar into a preserving pan and heat gently, stirring from time to time, until dissolved. Bring to the boil, then boil rapidly until setting point is reached (5–15 minutes). Skim with a draining spoon or stir in butter, if needed.

Wait for 5 minutes before ladling the fruit into the jars to prevent the fruit from rising in the jar. Ladle into warm, dry jars, filling to the very top, then cover with screw-top lids, or with waxed discs and cellophane tops secured with elastic bands. Label and leave to cool.

For strawberry & lavender jam, stir 3 teaspoons dried lavender petals into the cooked jam after skimming.

spiced plum jam

Makes **4–5 jars**
Preparation time **25 minutes**
Cooking time **50–55 minutes**

1.5 kg (3 lb) **just-ripe plums**,
  halved and stoned
grated rind and juice of
  1 orange
300 ml (½ pint) **water**
1 **cinnamon stick**, halved
1 teaspoon **whole cloves**
1.5 kg (3 lb) **granulated
  sugar**, warmed
15 g (½ oz) **butter** (optional)

Add the plums, orange rind and juice and measurement water to a preserving pan. Tie the cinnamon stick and cloves in muslin, then add to the preserving pan. Cover and cook gently for 30 minutes, until the plums are softened.

Pour the sugar into the pan and heat gently, stirring from time to time, until dissolved. Bring to the boil, then boil rapidly until setting point is reached (20–25 minutes). Discard the bag of spices. Skim the jam with a draining spoon or stir in butter, if needed.

Ladle into warm, dry jars, filling to the very top. Cover with screw-top lids, or with waxed discs and cellophane tops secured with elastic bands. Label and leave to cool.

To serve, this jam is delicious in sweet bread rolls with whipped cream, often called Devonshire splits.

For spiced greengage jam, make as above using 1.5 kg (3 lb) halved and stoned greengages instead of the plums.

cranberry, apple & orange jam

Makes **8 jars**
Preparation time **25 minutes**
Cooking time **40–45 minutes**

2 x 300 g (10 oz) packs **fresh**
or **frozen cranberries**
1.5 kg (3 lb) **cooking apples**,
peeled, cored and diced
grated rind and juice of
2 **oranges**, shells reserved
2 kg (4 lb) **granulated sugar**,
warmed
15 g (½ oz) **butter** (optional)

Add the cranberries, apples and orange rind to a preserving pan, orange shells and any pips tied in muslin. Make the orange juice up to 300 ml (½ pint) with water then add to the preserving pan. Cover and simmer gently for 30 minutes, stirring from time to time, until the fruit is tender.

Pour the sugar into the pan and heat gently, stirring from time to time, until dissolved. Bring to the boil, then boil rapidly until setting point is reached (10–15 minutes). Squeeze the muslin bag between two wooden spoons to extract as much juice as possible, then discard. Skim with a draining spoon or stir in the butter, if needed.

Ladle into warm, dry jars, filling to the very top. Cover with screw-top lids, or with waxed discs and cellophane tops secured in place with elastic bands. Label and leave to cool.

To serve, try spreading the jam liberally on buttered, toasted bagels.

For blackberry, apple & cinnamon jam, add 600 g (1¼ lb) blackberries and 1.5 kg (3 lb) peeled, cored and diced cooking apples to a preserving pan with a 7.5 cm (3 inch) cinnamon stick, halved, and the grated rind of 2 lemons. Make the juice of 2 lemons up to 300 ml (½ pint) with water, add to the pan, cover and cook for 30 minutes. Add the sugar and continue as above.

blueberry & honey jam

Makes **3 assorted jars**
Preparation time **10 minutes**
Cooking time **20–25 minutes**

600 g (1 ¼ lb) **blueberries**
150 ml (¼ pint) **water**
375 g (12 oz) **jam sugar**
  with pectin
125 g (4 oz) **clear honey**
juice of **1 lemon**
15 g (½ oz) **butter** (optional)

Add the blueberries and measurement water to a preserving pan and cook gently for 10 minutes, until softened, crushing from time to time with a wooden spoon or potato masher.

Add the sugar (no need to warm such a small quantity first), honey and lemon juice and heat gently, stirring from time to time, until dissolved. Bring to the boil, then boil rapidly until setting point is reached (10–15 minutes).

Skim with a draining spoon or stir in butter, if needed. Ladle into warm, dry jars, filling to the very top. Cover with screw-top lids, or with waxed discs and cellophane tops secured with elastic bands. Label and leave to cool.

To serve, a spoonful of this jam and a dollop of whipped cream makes a tasty addition to porridge.

For raspberry & honey jam, add 600 g (1 ¼ lb) raspberries and 150 ml (¼ pint) water to a preserving pan. Cook as above, then boil with sugar and honey. Continue as above.

black & redcurrant jam

Makes **4 jars**
Preparation time **15 minutes**
Cooking time **40–50 minutes**

500 g (1 lb) **redcurrants**
500 g (1 lb) **blackcurrants**
250 ml (8 fl oz) **water**
1 kg (2 lb) **granulated sugar**,
   warmed
15 g (½ oz) **butter** (optional)

Strip the currants from the stalks, then add to a preserving pan. Break up the fruit with a wooden spoon or potato masher, then add the measurement water. Cover and cook gently for 20–30 minutes, until the fruit is soft.

Pour the sugar into the pan and heat gently, stirring from time to time, until dissolved. Bring to the boil, then boil rapidly, stirring from time to time, until setting point is reached (about 20 minutes). Skim with a draining spoon or stir in butter if needed.

Ladle into warm, dry jars, filling to the very top, then cover with screw-top lids, or with waxed discs and cellophane tops secured with elastic bands. Label and leave to cool.

To serve, this jam is perfect for spooning over individual pavlovas topped with whipped cream.

For elderberry & blackberry jam, strip 500 g (1 lb) elderberries from their stalks and add to a preserving pan with 500 g (1 lb) blackberries and 150 ml (¼ pint) water. Cover and cook for 20–30 minutes, stirring and mashing with a potato masher, until the fruit is soft. Add 4 tablespoons lemon juice and 1 kg (2 lb) granulated sugar and continue as above.

fresh fig & blackberry jam

Makes **4 jars**
Preparation time **20 minutes**
Cooking time **35 minutes**

500 g (1 lb) **blackberries**
500 g (1 lb) **figs** (about 9),
  quartered
300 ml (½ pint) **water**
2 **cinnamon sticks**, halved
1 kg (2 lb) **granulated sugar**,
  warmed
juice of **1 lemon**
15 g (½ oz) **butter** (optional)

Add the blackberries and figs to a preserving pan. Pour in the measurement water, then add the cinnamon sticks. Bring to a simmer, then simmer, uncovered, for about 10 minutes, until the fruit is just beginning to soften.

Pour the sugar into the pan and add the lemon juice. Heat gently, stirring from time to time, until the sugar has dissolved. Bring to the boil, then boil rapidly until setting point is reached (about 25 minutes). Skim with a draining spoon or stir in butter if needed.

Ladle into warm, dry jars, filling to the very top and discarding the cinnamon sticks. Cover with screw-top lids, or with waxed discs and cellophane tops secured with elastic bands. Label and leave to cool.

For gingered blackberry & fig jam, omit the cinnamon sticks and add a 3.5 cm (1½ inch) piece of root ginger, peeled and finely chopped.

orchard fruit jam

Makes **5 jars**
Preparation time **25 minutes**
Cooking time **40–45 minutes**

500 g (1 lb) **plums**, halved
   and stoned
500 g (1 lb) **pears**, quartered,
   cored, peeled and diced
500 g (1 lb) **cooking apples**,
   quartered, cored, peeled
   and diced
300 ml (½ pint) **water**
1.5 kg (3 lb) **granulated
   sugar**, warmed
15 g (½ oz) **butter** (optional)

Add the fruit to a preserving pan with the measurement water. Cover and cook gently for 20 minutes, stirring from time to time, until the fruit is just beginning to soften.

Pour the sugar into the pan and heat gently, stirring from time to time, until dissolved. Bring to the boil, then boil rapidly until setting point is reached (20–25 minutes). Skim with a draining spoon or stir in butter if needed.

Ladle into warm, dry jars, filling to the very top. Cover with screw-top lids, or with waxed discs and cellophane tops secured with elastic bands. Label and leave to cool.

To serve, this jam can be used as the filling between 2 shortbread biscuits, the top layer having a small heart shape cut out before baking.

For apple & blackberry jam, cook 750 g (1 ½ lb) cooking apples, quartered, cored, peeled and diced, with 750 g (1 ½ lb) blackberries in 300 ml (½ pint) water, then continue as above.

pineapple & passion fruit jam

Makes **4–5 jars**

Preparation time **15 minutes**

Cooking time **1 hour
40 minutes–1 hour
50 minutes**

1 large ripe **pineapple**

750 g (1½ lb) **cooking
apples**, roughly chopped

6 **passion fruits**, quartered

1.2 litres (2 pints) **water**

1.5 kg (3 lb) **granulated
sugar**, warmed

juice of 2 large **lemons**

15 g (½ oz) **butter** (optional)

Peel the pineapple and roughly chop the peel together with any leaves. Put the chopped peel and leaves into a preserving pan with the apples and passion fruits and pour in the measurement water. Bring to the boil, then reduce the heat, cover the pan and simmer for 1 hour.

Meanwhile, chop the pineapple flesh, cutting up the hard core more finely than the soft part of the fruit. Set aside.

Press the cooked pulp through a fine sieve, pour the resulting purée back into the pan and add the fresh pineapple. Bring the fruit mixture slowly to the boil, then reduce the heat to a simmer, cover the pan and cook the fruit for 30 minutes, until quite tender.

Add the sugar and lemon juice and cook over a low heat, stirring continuously, until the sugar has completely dissolved. Bring to the boil, then boil rapidly until setting point is reached (10–20 minutes). Remove from the heat and skim with a draining spoon or stir in butter if needed.

Ladle into warm, dry jars. Cover with screw-top lids, or with waxed discs and cellophane tops secured with elastic bands. Label and leave to cool.

For gingered pineapple & sultana jam, cook as above, adding a 4 cm (1½ inch) piece of peeled and finely chopped root ginger and 100 g (3½ oz) sultanas along with the sugar.

plum, marrow & blackberry jam

Makes **6 jars**
Preparation time **25 minutes**
Cooking time **35–40 minutes**

1 small **marrow**, 750–875 g
  (1½–1¾ lb), peeled, halved,
  deseeded and diced
1.5 kg (3 lb) **just ripe plums**,
  quartered and stoned
250 g (8 oz) **blackberries**
300 ml (½ pint) **water**
1.5 kg (3 lb) **granulated
  sugar**, warmed
15 g (½ oz) **butter** (optional)

Add the marrow, plums and blackberries to a preserving pan with the measurement water, then cover and cook for 20 minutes, until the fruits are just tender.

Pour the sugar into the pan and heat gently, stirring from time to time, until dissolved. Bring to the boil, then boil rapidly until setting point is reached (15–20 minutes). Skim with a draining spoon or stir in butter if needed.

Ladle into warm, dry jars, filling to the very top. Cover with screw-top lids, or with waxed discs and cellophane tops secured with elastic bands. Label and leave to cool.

To serve, this jam is delicious simply eaten with bread and butter.

For apple, marrow & ginger jam, add 1.75 kg (3½ lb) quartered, cored and diced cooking apples to 1 prepared marrow. Add the grated rind and juice of 2 lemons and 100 g (3½ oz) drained and finely chopped stem ginger in place of the blackberries. Cook in 300 ml (½ pint) water and continue as above.

raspberry & redcurrant jam

Makes **4 jars**
Preparation time **5 minutes**
Cooking time **30–40 minutes**

500 g (1 lb) **raspberries**
500 g (1 lb) **redcurrants**
300 ml (½ pint) **water**
juice of 2 **lemons**
1 kg (2 lb) **granulated sugar,**
  warmed
15 g (½ oz) **butter** (optional)

Add the fruit to a preserving pan with the measurement water. Bring to the boil, then reduce the heat and cover the pan. Simmer for 20–30 minutes, until the redcurrants are really tender.

Add the lemon juice and sugar and stir over a low heat until the sugar has completely dissolved.

Increase the heat and bring to the boil, then boil rapidly until setting point is reached (10–20 minutes). Remove the pan from the heat and skim with a draining spoon or stir in butter if needed.

Ladle into warm, dry jars. Cover with screw-top lids, or with waxed discs and cellophane tops secured with elastic bands. Label and leave to cool.

To serve, spoon over split scones topped with whipped or clotted cream.

For gooseberry & strawberry jam, add 500 g (1 lb) gooseberries to a preserving pan with 150 ml (¼ pint) water, cover and cook gently for 15 minutes, until soft. Add 500 g (1 lb) strawberries, cook for a further 10 minutes, mashing the strawberries with a potato masher, until soft. Add 1 kg (2 lb) granulated sugar, then continue as above. (No need to add lemon juice.)

mango & passion fruit jam

Makes **5 jars**
Preparation time **30 minutes**
Cooking time **18–30 minutes**

2 kg (4 lb) ripe mangoes
(about 3 large ones)
grated rind and juice of
3 large **limes**
125 ml (4 fl oz) **water**
1 kg (2 lb) **granulated sugar,**
warmed
3 **passion fruits**, halved

Cut a thick slice off either side of each mango to reveal the large, flattish stone. Trim the flesh from around the stone, then cut away the peel, dice the flesh and add to a preserving pan. Cut criss-cross lines over the remaining mango slices, then press the skin side so that the squares of mango stand proud of the skin, like a hedgehog. Slide a knife under the cubes of mango to release, and add to the pan with the lime juice and measurement water.

Cook, uncovered, over a low heat for 8–10 minutes, stirring from time to time, until the mango is soft.

Add the lime rind and sugar and heat gently, stirring from time to time, until the sugar has completely dissolved. Bring to the boil, then boil rapidly until setting point is reached (10–20 minutes).

Turn off the heat, scoop the passion fruit seeds from the fruit with a teaspoon and stir into the jam. Allow to cool for 5–10 minutes so that the seeds will not rise in the jam, then spoon into warm, dry jars, filling to the very top. Cover with screw-top lids, or with waxed discs and cellophane tops secured with elastic bands. Label and leave to cool.

For papaya & lime jam, halve 3 large ripe papayas, remove and discard the black seeds, then peel and dice the fruit. Add to a preserving pan with the grated rind and juice of 6 large limes and 120 ml (4 fl oz) water, mash the papaya from time to time as it cooks with the lime rind and juice and water, and continue as above.

cherry & raspberry jam

Makes **4–5 assorted jars**
Preparation time **20 minutes**
Cooking time **15–20 minutes**

2 x 480 g (15¼ oz) packs
frozen pitted cherries
340 g (12 oz) **fresh**
raspberries
1 kg (2 lb) **jam sugar**
with pectin
15 g (½ oz) **butter** (optional)

Add the frozen cherries and the raspberries to a preserving pan. Cover and cook gently for 10 minutes, stirring from time to time, until the juices run and the fruit begins to soften.

Pour the sugar into the pan and heat gently, stirring from time to time, until dissolved. Bring to the boil, then boil rapidly until setting point is reached (5–10 minutes). Skim with a draining spoon or stir in butter if needed.

Leave to cool for 10 minutes so that the cherries don't rise in the jars, then ladle into warm, dry jars, filling to the very top. Cover with screw-top lids, or with waxed discs and cellophane tops secured with elastic bands. Label and leave to cool.

For blueberry & raspberry jam, omit the frozen cherries and add the same weight of frozen blueberries. Cook with the fresh raspberries and continue as above.

chestnut jam with whisky

Makes **2 small jars**
Preparation time **15 minutes**
Cooking time **50 minutes**

625 g (1¼ lb) **cooked,
    peeled chestnuts**
1 **vanilla pod**
375 g (12 oz) **soft light
    brown sugar**
2 tablespoons **whisky**

Put the chestnuts and vanilla pod into a heavy-based pan and add enough water to just cover them. Bring to the boil, then reduce the heat, cover the pan and simmer for 30 minutes. Remove the vanilla pod and set aside, then strain and reserve the cooking liquid. Purée the chestnuts in a food processor or blender, adding a little of the reserved liquid if necessary.

Put the chestnut purée back into the pan. Slice the vanilla pod lengthways and scrape the seeds into the pan.

Add the sugar and 75 ml (3 fl oz) of the cooking liquid and stir to blend. Bring to the boil, stirring frequently, and cook for about 5 minutes, or until very thick. Remove from the heat and add the whisky.

Ladle into warm, dry jars. Cover with screw-top lids, or with waxed discs and cellophane tops secured with elastic bands. Label and leave to mature for 2 days in a cool, dark place.

To serve, layer spoonfuls of jam in small glasses with honey-flavoured natural yogurt.

For chestnut, cinnamon & orange jam, cook the chestnuts in water as above but omit the vanilla. Purée, then mix with the grated rind and juice of 1 large orange, 1 teaspoon ground cinnamon and 375 g (12 oz) soft light brown sugar. Cook as above, then stir in 2 tablespoons Grand Marnier or Cointreau instead of the whisky.

strawberry champagne conserve

Makes **5–6 jars**
Preparation time **10 minutes,
   plus standing**
Cooking time **15–20 minutes**

1.5 kg (3 lb) **strawberries**,
   hulled or quartered,
   depending on size
1.5 kg (3 lb) **jam sugar
   with pectin**
150 ml (¼ pint) or 1 glass **dry
   Champagne** or **sparkling
   white wine**
1½ teaspoons **citric acid**
15 g (½ oz) **butter** (optional)

Add half the strawberries to a preserving pan and crush them roughly with a potato masher.

Add the sugar, the remaining strawberries, the Champagne or wine and citric acid and heat gently for 10 minutes, stirring continuously, until the sugar has completely dissolved.

Increase the heat and boil rapidly for 5–10 minutes, testing at 5-minute intervals, until setting point is reached. Skim with a draining spoon or stir in butter if needed, then remove from the heat and leave the conserve to stand for 15 minutes to allow the fruit to settle.

Ladle into warm, dry jars. Cover with screw-top lids, or with waxed discs and cellophane tops secured with elastic bands. Label and store in a cool, dark place.

To serve, spread over hot, buttered crumpets.

For lychee & strawberry conserve, peel and stone fresh lychees, then weigh them – you will need 500 g (1 lb). Add to a preserving pan with 1 kg (2 lb) hulled strawberries and roughly crush with a potato masher. Add the sugar and citric acid, then 150 ml (¼ pint) water in place of the Champagne, and continue as above.

peach & vanilla conserve

Makes **3 jars**
Preparation time **20 minutes**
Cooking time **25–30 minutes**

1 kg (2 lb) **ripe peaches**,
  halved, stoned and diced
1 kg (2 lb) **jam sugar**
  with pectin
juice of 1 large **lemon**
1 **vanilla pod**
15 g (½ oz) **butter** (optional)

Add the peaches, sugar and lemon juice to a preserving pan. Slit the vanilla pod lengthways, then scrape out the seeds and add to the pan. Cut the pod into very thin strips, and add this to the pan. Cook very gently, uncovered, for 20 minutes, until the peaches are tender and the sugar has dissolved to make a syrup, stirring from time to time.

Bring to the boil, then boil rapidly until setting point is reached (5–10 minutes). Skim with a draining spoon or stir in butter if needed.

Leave the conserve to stand for 5–10 minutes so that the fruit will not rise in the jars, then ladle into warm, dry jars, filling to the very top. Cover with screw-top lids, or with waxed discs and cellophane tops secured with elastic bands. Label and leave to cool.

For apricot & vodka conserve, halve, stone and dice 1 kg (2 lb) fresh apricots and add to the preserving pan with 1 kg (2 lb) jam sugar with pectin and the juice of 1 large lemon. Cook as above, then boil until setting point is reached. Stir in 4 tablespoons vodka, cook for 1 minute, then pot as above.

pineapple & kiwi conserve

Makes **3 jars**
Preparation time **25 minutes**
Cooking time **25–35 minutes**

1 large **pineapple**, trimmed,
  peeled and cored
grated rind of 2 **limes**
125 ml (4 fl oz) freshly
  squeezed **lime juice**
  (about 3 limes)
4 **kiwi fruits**, peeled and
  thinly sliced
750 g (1½ lb) **granulated
  sugar**, warmed
15 g (½ oz) **butter** (optional)

Dice half the pineapple, then finely chop the remainder in a food processor. Add the diced and crushed pineapple, lime rind and juice to a preserving pan, then cover and cook very gently for 10 minutes. Add the kiwi fruits and cook for 5 minutes, until the fruit has softened.

Pour in the sugar and heat gently, stirring from time to time, until dissolved. Bring to the boil, then boil rapidly until setting point is reached (10–20 minutes). Skim with a draining spoon or stir in butter if needed.

Ladle into warm, dry jars, filling to the very top. Cover with screw-top lids, or with waxed discs and cellophane tops secured with elastic bands. Label and leave to cool.

To serve, this conserve is lovely with toast and butter.

For pineapple & pomegranate conserve, omit the kiwi fruits and stir the seeds from 1 pomegranate into the conserve just as it comes up to setting point. Continue cooking until setting point is reached and continue as above.

peach melba conserve

Makes **7 jars**
Preparation time **25 minutes**
Cooking time **20–25 minutes**

1.5 kg (3 lb) **peaches**, halved,
   stoned and diced
grated rind and juice of
   2 **lemons**
200 ml (7 fl oz) **water**
250 g (½ lb) **raspberries**
1.75 kg (3½ lb) **jam sugar**
   with pectin
15 g (½ oz) **butter** (optional)

Add the peaches to a preserving pan with the lemon rind
and juice and measurement water. Cover and cook gently
for 15 minutes, until the peaches are just softened.

Add the raspberries with the sugar and cook gently,
stirring from time to time, until the sugar has dissolved.
Bring to the boil, then boil rapidly until setting point is
reached (5–10 minutes). Skim with a draining spoon
or stir in butter if needed.

Ladle into warm, dry jars, filling to the very top. Cover
with screw-top lids, or with waxed discs and cellophane
tops secured with elastic bands. Label and leave to cool.

To serve, this conserve goes well with vanilla ice cream
and sliced peaches.

For peach jam, make as above using 1.75 kg (3½ lb)
peaches instead of the peaches and raspberries.

cheat's tropical fruit conserve

Makes **4–5 assorted jars**
Preparation time **20 minutes**
Cooking time **20–25 minutes**

3 x 480 g (15¼ oz) bags
   **frozen ready-prepared
   tropical fruit,** including
   pineapple, mango, papaya,
   kiwi and pomegranate seeds
grated rind and juice of
   2 large **limes**
1 kg (2 lb) **jam sugar
   with pectin**
15 g (½ oz) **butter** (optional)

Add the frozen fruit to a preserving pan with the lime rind and juice. Cover and cook gently for 10 minutes, stirring from time to time, until the juices begin to run.

Roughly chop the fruit while still in the preserving pan, using a knife and fork, if the pieces are very large. Pour in the sugar and heat gently, stirring from time to time, until dissolved. Bring to the boil, and boil rapidly until setting point is reached (10–15 minutes). Skim with a draining spoon or stir in butter if needed.

Leave to cool for 10 minutes so that the fruit doesn't rise in the jars, then ladle into warm, dry jars, filling to the very top and pressing any larger pieces of fruit below the jam. Cover with screw-top lids, or with waxed discs and cellophane tops secured with elastic bands. Label and leave to cool.

For cheat's fruits of the forest jam, use 3 x 500 g (1 lb) bags mixed frozen berries and cherries, cook with the grated rind and juice of 2 lemons, then add sugar and continue as above.

no-cook strawberry conserve

Makes **6 pots**

Preparation time **20 minutes, plus standing and freezing**

600 g (1 ¼ lb) **strawberries**, hulled and sliced

1 kg (2 lb) **caster sugar**

4 tablespoons freshly squeezed **lemon juice** (about 2 lemons)

150 ml (¼ pint) **liquid pectin**

Crush the strawberries with a potato masher, or by blending briefly in a food processor using the pulse setting so that there are pieces of strawberry rather than a fine purée. Add to a large bowl and stir in the sugar, then cover and leave to stand for 1 ½–2 hours, stirring from time to time, until the sugar has dissolved.

Stir in the lemon juice, then add the pectin and continue stirring for 2 minutes. Ladle into small clear plastic pots leaving a gap of 1 cm (½ inch) at the top. Clip or press on lids. Label and leave at room temperature overnight for the conserve to 'gel'.

Transfer to the freezer to store until required. Defrost overnight in the refrigerator, then transfer to attractive jars and serve in the same way as a conventional jam.

For no-cook raspberry conserve, make using 600 g (1 ¼ lb) roughly crushed raspberries, then mix with the sugar and continue as above.

reduced-sugar apricot conserve

Makes **2 jars**
Preparation time **25 minutes**
Cooking time **35–40 minutes**

750 g (1½lb) **dessert apples**
   (about 5), quartered, cored,
   peeled and diced
250 g (8 oz) **ready-to-eat
   dried apricots**, diced
450 ml (¾ pint) **water**
2 tablespoons **Greek or other
   strong-flavoured honey**

Add the apples, apricots and measurement water to a preserving pan, then drizzle over the honey. Cover and cook gently for 30 minutes, stirring and mashing the fruit from time to time with a fork, until soft.

Remove the lid and cook for a further 5–10 minutes, stirring frequently, until very thick and jam-like. As this jam has only a little honey, it is more like a chutney in consistency and doesn't need to be tested for setting.

Ladle into warm, dry jars, packing the fruit down well, dispersing any air pockets with a small knife or skewer and filling to the very top of the jars. Cover with screw-top lids, leave to cool and store in the refrigerator for up to 10 days.

For reduced-sugar apricot, date & apple conserve, prepare 750 g (1½ lb) dessert apples and add to a preserving pan with 125 g (4 oz) diced dates (don't use ready-diced dates coated in sugar) and 125 g (4 oz) diced ready-to-eat dried apricots. Cook with water and honey plus 2 teaspoons ground cinnamon and continue as above.

green grape conserve

Makes **2 jars**
Preparation time **20 minutes**
Cooking time **10–20 minutes**

1 kg (2 lb) **seedless
  green grapes**
grated rind and juice of
  1 lemon
6 tablespoons **water**
500 g (1 lb) **granulated
  sugar**, warmed
15 g (½ oz) **butter** (optional)

Wash the grapes and pick off the bunch, carefully removing the stalks. Add the fruit to the preserving pan with the lemon rind and juice and the measurement water. Cover and simmer gently for 10 minutes, until the juices have run and the fruit has softened.

Roughly mash the grapes with a potato masher, then add the warmed sugar and cook gently, stirring from time to time, until the sugar has completely dissolved. Bring to the boil and cook until setting point is reached (10–20 minutes). Skim with a draining spoon or stir in butter if needed.

Leave to cool for 10 minutes so that the grapes don't rise in the jars, then ladle into warm, dry jars, filling to the very top. Cover with screw-top lids, or with waxed discs and cellophane tops secured with elastic bands. Label and leave to cool.

To serve, this conserve tastes good with rustic bread and butter.

For green grape & almond jam, cook the grapes as above with the grated rind and juice of 1 lemon plus the grated rind of 1 small orange and 6 tablespoons water. Add the sugar, as above. When the jam has reached setting point, stir in 3 tablespoons flaked almonds, then pot as above.

mixed summer berry conserve

Makes **6 jars**
Preparation time **20 minutes**
Cooking time **40–50 minutes**

500 g (1 lb) **redcurrants**,
   stripped from stalks
juice of **1 lemon**
150 ml (¼ pint) **water**
500 g (1 lb) **strawberries**,
   hulled and halved if large
500 g (1 lb) **raspberries**
1.5 kg (3 lb) **granulated**
   sugar, warmed
15 g (½ oz) **butter** (optional)

Add the redcurrants to a preserving pan and roughly crush with a potato masher. Add the lemon juice and measurement water, cover and cook gently for 20–25 minutes, until soft.

Stir in the strawberries and raspberries, then cook for 5 minutes, until just beginning to soften.

Pour the sugar into the pan and heat gently, stirring from time to time, until dissolved. Bring to the boil, then boil rapidly until setting point is reached (20–25 minutes). Skim with a draining spoon or stir in butter if needed.

Ladle into warm, dry jars, filling to the very top. Cover with screw-top lids, or with waxed discs and cellophane tops secured with elastic bands. Label and leave to cool.

To serve, this jam makes an excellent topping for individual steamed sponge puddings.

For frozen berry jam, gently heat 3 x 500 g (1 lb) packs frozen mixed summer berries in a preserving pan (no need to add any water), until the juice begins to run and the fruit defrosts, then continue to cook for 10 minutes. Add the juice of 1 lemon and 1.5 kg (3 lb) granulated sugar, and continue as above.

banana & chocolate jam

Makes **3 assorted jars**
Preparation time **20 minutes**
Cooking time **8–10 minutes**

1 kg (2 lb) **bananas**, peeled
  and sliced
juice of 1 **lemon**
250 ml (8 fl oz) **water**
500 g (1 lb) **jam sugar**
  with pectin
100 g (3½ oz) **dark chocolate**,
  broken into pieces

Add the bananas and lemon juice to a preserving pan and toss together. Add the measurement water, then cook gently, uncovered, for 5 minutes, until the bananas are just beginning to soften.

Pour the sugar into the pan and heat gently, stirring from time to time, until dissolved. Bring to the boil, then boil for 3–5 minutes until very thick and the jam slowly drops from a spoon. As this jam thickens so quickly, test for a set with a spoon rather than a sugar thermometer or wrinkle test on a saucer.

Turn off the heat and stir in the chocolate. Ladle into warm, dry jars, filling to the very top. Cover with screw-top lids, or with waxed discs and cellophane tops secured with elastic bands. Store in the refrigerator.

To serve, this jam can be spread over crepes and dusted with icing sugar.

For banana & date jam, omit the chocolate and add 100 (3½ oz) stoned and chopped dates and 1 teaspoon ground ginger when cooking the bananas. Continue as above.

fruit butters, curds & cheeses

apple, apricot & elderflower butter

Makes **3 jars**
Preparation time **30 minutes**
Cooking time **1 hour**
  25 minutes–1 hour
  30 minutes

1 kg (2 lb) **cooking apples**,
  quartered, cored, peeled
  and diced
250 g (8 oz) **ready-to-eat**
  dried apricots, diced
1 **lemon**, finely chopped,
  including pith and peel
600 ml (1 pint) **water**
about 600 g (1¼ lb)
  granulated sugar
15 g (½ oz) **butter** (optional)
3 tablespoons **undiluted**
  elderflower cordial

Add the apples, apricots, lemon and measurement water to a preserving pan. Cover and simmer gently for 1 hour, stirring from time to time, until the fruit is soft.

Purée the fruit in batches in a food processor or liquidizer with the cooking water, or press through a sieve. Weigh the purée, then return to the preserving pan. For every 500 g (1 lb) of purée add 250 g (8 oz) sugar.

Heat gently, stirring from time to time, until the sugar has dissolved, then increase the heat to medium and cook for 25–30 minutes, stirring more frequently towards the end of cooking until the fruit mixture has darkened slightly to a rich amber, is thick, creamy and glossy and drops slowly from a wooden spoon. Skim with a draining spoon or stir in butter if needed.

Stir in the elderflower cordial. Ladle into warm, dry jars, filling to the very top. Cover with screw-top lids, or with waxed discs and cellophane tops secured with elastic bands. Label and leave to cool.

For apple, prune & vanilla butter, add 250 g (8 oz) ready-to-eat stoned prunes instead of the apricots and flavour with 2 teaspoons vanilla extract instead of the elderflower cordial. Continue as above.

pear & strawberry butter

Makes **2–3 assorted jars**
Preparation time **25 minutes**
Cooking time **55–60 minutes**

750 g (1½ lb) **pears**, quartered,
    cored, peeled and sliced
juice of **1 lemon**
750 g (1½ lb) **strawberries**,
    hulled and sliced
600 ml (1 pint) **water**
about 750 g (1½ lb)
    granulated sugar
15 g (½ oz) **butter** (optional)

Add the pears and lemon juice to a preserving pan and toss together, then add the strawberries and measurement water. Cover and simmer gently for 30 minutes, stirring from time to time, until the fruit is soft and pulpy.

Purée the fruit in batches in a food processor or liquidizer with the cooking water or press through a sieve. Weigh the purée, then return to the preserving pan. For every 500 g (1 lb) of purée add 250 g (8 oz) sugar.

Heat gently, stirring from time to time, until the sugar has dissolved, then increase the heat to medium and cook for 25–30 minutes, stirring more frequently towards the end of cooking, until the fruit mixture has darkened very slightly, is thick, creamy and glossy and drops slowly from a wooden spoon. Skim with a draining spoon or stir in butter if needed.

Ladle into warm, dry jars, filling to the very top. Cover with screw-top lids, or with waxed discs and cellophane tops secured with elastic bands. Label and leave to cool.

For pear & plum butter, replace the strawberries with 750 g (1½ lb) stoned plums and cook with water as above.

cranberry & cinnamon butter

Makes **6 jars**
Preparation time **25 minutes**
Cooking time **1 hour–**
  1 hour 10 minutes

1.25 kg (2½ lb) **cranberries**,
  fresh or frozen
1 litre (1¾ pint) **water**
rind of 2 **oranges**
about 1.5 kg (3 lb)
  granulated sugar
2 teaspoons **ground**
  cinnamon
15 g (½ oz) **butter** (optional)

Add the cranberries to a preserving pan; if they are frozen there is no need to defrost first. Pour over the measurement water, then add the orange rind and bring to the boil. Cover and simmer gently for 30 minutes, stirring from time to time, and breaking up with a wooden spoon or potato masher until the cranberries are very soft.

Leave the cranberries to cool slightly. Purée in small batches in a food processor or liquidizer or press through a sieve. Weigh the purée and return to the rinsed preserving pan. For every 500 g (1 lb) of purée add 375 g (12 oz) sugar with the ground cinnamon.

Heat gently, stirring from time to time, until the sugar has dissolved, then increase the heat to medium and cook for 30–40 minutes, stirring more frequently towards the end of cooking, until the mixture has reduced almost by half, is slightly darker in colour, is thick and glossy and drops slowly from a wooden spoon. Skim with a draining spoon or stir in butter, if needed.

Ladle into warm, dry jars, filling to the very top. Cover with screw-top lids, or with waxed discs and cellophane tops secured with elastic bands. Label and leave to cool.

For cranberry & pear butter, use 875 g (1¾ lb) cranberries and 2 peeled, cored and diced pears. Cook with the rind and juice of 2 oranges and 900 ml (1½ pints) water. Continue as above, omitting the cinnamon.

72

spiced apple butter

Makes **3–4 jars**
Preparation time **20 minutes**
Cooking time **1½ hours**

1.25 kg (2½ lb) **cooking
  apples**, roughly chopped
1 **cinnamon stick**
1 teaspoon **freshly grated
  nutmeg**
1 **lemon**, chopped
600 ml (1 pint) **water**
about 625 g (1¼ lb)
  granulated sugar

Add the apples, spices, chopped lemon and measurement water to a preserving pan. Bring to the boil, then reduce the heat and simmer, covered, for 1 hour, or until the fruit is reduced to a pulp.

Purée in small batches in a food processor or liquidizer. Press the mixture through a fine sieve, then weigh the resulting purée and put it into a clean pan. For every 500 g (1 lb) of purée add 375 g (12 oz) sugar and cook over a low heat, stirring continuously, until the sugar has completely dissolved. Increase the heat to medium, then cook for about 30 minutes, stirring frequently, until the mixture is reduced by half and is thick and glossy and falls slowly from a wooden spoon.

Ladle into warm, dry jars, filling to the very top. Cover with screw-top lids, or with waxed discs and cellophane tops secured with elastic bands. Label and leave to cool.

To serve, enjoy this preserve with cheese and biscuits.

For apple & ginger wine butter, roughly chop 1.25 kg (2½ lb) cooking apples and add to a preserving pan with 1 roughly chopped lemon. Cook with 450 ml (¾ pint) water and 150 ml (¼ pint) ginger wine as above, then sieve and finish with the sugar.

spiced pumpkin butter

Makes **3 small jars**
Preparation time **30 minutes**
Cooking time **30 minutes**

1.25 kg (2½ lb) **ready-
prepared pumpkin**, weighed
after peel and seeds have
been removed
about 400 g (13 oz)
granulated sugar
1 teaspoon **ground ginger**
1 teaspoon **ground
mixed spice**
75 g (3 oz) **stem ginger**
in syrup, drained and
finely chopped
15 g (½ oz) **butter** (optional)

Cut the pumpkin into pieces about 1.5 cm (¾ inch) square, then steam for about 15 minutes until tender.

Leave to cool slightly, then purée in a liquidizer or food processor or press through a sieve until smooth. Weigh the purée, then pour into a preserving pan. For every 500 g (1 lb) of purée add 250 g (8 oz) sugar.

Stir in the spices and ginger, then heat gently, stirring from time to time, until the sugar has dissolved. Increase the heat to medium and cook for about 15 minutes, stirring more frequently towards the end of cooking until the fruit mixture has darkened slightly, is thick, creamy and glossy and drops slowly from a wooden spoon. Skim with a draining spoon or stir in butter if needed.

Ladle into warm, dry jars, filling to the very top. Cover with screw-top lids, or with waxed discs and cellophane tops secured with elastic bands. Label and leave to cool.

To serve, this butter can be used in tiny lattice-topped tarts to make baby pumpkin pies.

For pumpkin & muscovado butter, replace the granulated sugar with light muscovado sugar. Stir in the ground spices but omit the chopped ginger. Continue as above.

st clement's curd

Makes **2 jars**
Preparation time **25 minutes**
Cooking time **40–50 minutes**

125 g (4 oz) **butter**, diced
400 g (13 oz) **caster sugar**
grated rind and juice of
  2 **lemons**
grated rind and juice of
  1 **orange**
grated rind and juice of 1 **lime**
4 **eggs**, beaten

Heat the butter in a large bowl set over a saucepan of simmering water until melted.

Pour the sugar into the melted butter, then add the grated fruit rinds. Strain in the fruit juices, discarding any pips, then strain in the beaten eggs and mix together. Cook for 40–50 minutes, stirring from time to time, until the sugar has dissolved and the mixture has thickened.

Ladle into warm, dry jars, filling to the very top. Cover with screw-top lids, or with waxed discs and cellophane tops secured with elastic bands. Label and leave to cool. Store in the refrigerator for up to 2 weeks.

For traditional lemon curd, use the grated rind and juice of 3 large lemons in place of the lemons, orange and lime. Continue as above.

apple & ginger curd

Makes **3 assorted jars**
Preparation time **25 minutes**
Cooking time **55–65 minutes**

750 g (1½ lb) **cooking
    apples**, quartered, cored,
    peeled and diced
6 tablespoons **ginger wine**
grated rind and juice of
    1 lemon
125 g (4 oz) **butter**, diced
375 g (12 oz) **caster sugar**
3 **eggs**, beaten
50 g (2 oz) drained **stem
    ginger in syrup**, finely
    chopped

Add the apples, ginger wine, lemon rind and juice to a saucepan, then cover and cook gently for about 15 minutes, stirring from time to time, until the apples are soft. Leave to cool for 10–15 minutes.

Purée the apple mixture in a food processor or liquidizer or press through a sieve. Place the butter in a large bowl set over a saucepan of simmering water and warm until just melted.

Add the sugar and apple purée to the bowl, then strain in the eggs and cook over medium heat for 40–50 minutes, stirring frequently until the sugar has dissolved and the eggs have thickened the mixture (take care not to have the heat too high or the eggs will curdle).

Stir in the chopped ginger, then ladle into warm, dry jars, filling to the very top. Cover with screw-top lids, or with waxed discs and cellophane tops secured with elastic bands. Label and leave to cool. Store in the refrigerator for up to 2 weeks.

For spiced apple curd, cook the apples with 6 tablespoons water, the grated rind and juice of 1 lemon, 4 cloves and a 5 cm (2 inch) piece of cinnamon stick. Remove the spices, then purée. Continue as above, omitting the chopped ginger.

raspberry & red grapefruit curd

Makes **2 jars**
Preparation time **20 minutes**
Cooking time **40–50 minutes**

175 g (6 oz) **raspberries**
juice of **1 red grapefruit**
125 g (4 oz) **butter**, diced
375 g (12 oz) **caster sugar**
4 **eggs**, beaten
few drops **red food colouring**
   (optional)

Purée the raspberries with the grapefruit juice in a food processor or liquidizer until smooth, then press through a sieve and discard the raspberry seeds.

Heat the butter in a large bowl set over a saucepan of simmering water until melted. Stir in the sugar and raspberry purée, then strain in the eggs and mix together. Cook for 40–50 minutes, stirring from time to time, until the sugar has dissolved and mixture has thickened.

Stir in a few drops of food colouring, if liked, then ladle into warm, dry jars, filling to the very top. Cover with screw-top lids, or with waxed discs and cellophane tops secured with elastic bands. Label and leave to cool. Store in the refrigerator for up to 2 weeks.

To serve, this curd can be teamed with shortbread biscuits, whipped cream and whole raspberries for a dainty dessert.

For raspberry & lemon curd, omit the grapefruit juice and add the grated rind and juice of 2 lemons, adding the grated rind when mixing the fruit purée into the melted butter and sugar mix. Continue as above.

lime & passion fruit curd

Makes **2 jars**
Preparation time **15 minutes**
Cooking time **30–40 minutes**

250 g (8 oz) **caster sugar**
finely grated rind and juice
   of **4 limes**
125 g (4 oz) **unsalted butter**,
   cut into pieces
4 **eggs**, beaten
3 **passion fruits**

Heat the sugar and lime rind in a bowl set over a saucepan of simmering water, pressing the rind against the side of the bowl using a wooden spoon to release the oils.

Strain the lime juice into the bowl and add the butter. Heat, stirring occasionally, until the butter has melted. Strain the eggs into the mixture and mix together. Continue heating gently for 20–30 minutes, stirring from time to time, until the mixture is very thick. Remove the bowl from the heat.

Halve the passion fruits, then scoop the seeds into the lime curd. Mix together gently.

Ladle into warm, dry jars, filling to the very top. Cover with screw-top lids, or with waxed discs and cellophane tops secured with elastic bands. Store in the refrigerator for up to 2 weeks.

For lime & coconut curd, stir 4 tablespoons of desiccated coconut into the curd mixture after adding the strained eggs.

gooseberry curd

Makes **2 jars**
Preparation time **25 minutes**
Cooking time **55–60 minutes**

250 g (8 oz) **gooseberries**,
   topped and tailed
grated rind and juice of
   1 **lemon**
4 tablespoons **water**
125 g (4 oz) **butter**
400 g (13 oz) **caster sugar**
4 **eggs**, beaten
few drops **green food
   colouring** (optional)

Add the gooseberries, lemon rind and juice and measurement water to a medium saucepan, cover and cook gently for 15 minutes until the gooseberries are soft. Leave to cool slightly, then purée in a food processor or liquidizer and press through a sieve to remove the seeds.

Heat the butter in a large bowl set over a saucepan of simmering water until melted. Stir in the sugar and gooseberry purée, then strain in the eggs and mix together. Cook for 40–50 minutes, stirring from time to time, until the sugar has dissolved and the mixture has thickened.

Stir in a few drops of food colouring, if liked, then ladle into warm, dry jars, filling to the very top. Cover with screw-top lids, or with waxed discs and cellophane tops secured with elastic bands. Leave to cool. Store in the refrigerator for up to 2 weeks.

To serve, this curd tastes good with warmed croissants.

For gooseberry & elderflower curd, stir 3 tablespoons of undiluted elderflower cordial into the bowl when adding the eggs. Continue as above.

pear & red wine cheese

Makes **2 jars**
Preparation time **30 minutes**
Cooking time **1¼–1½ hours**

1.5 kg (3 lb) **pears**, quartered,
   cored, peeled and sliced
1 teaspoon **cloves**, roughly
   crushed
300 ml (½ pint) **red wine**
300 ml (½ pint) **water**
about 1.5 kg (3 lb)
   granulated sugar
15 g (½ oz) **butter**, optional

Add the pears and crushed cloves to a preserving pan. Pour over the wine and measurement water to just cover the base of the pan, then bring to the boil. Cover and cook gently for 30 minutes, stirring from time and breaking up the pears with a wooden spoon or potato masher, until very soft.

Allow to cool slightly, then purée in small batches in a food processor or liquidizer, or press through a sieve.

Weigh the purée, then pour back into the rinsed preserving pan. For every 500 g (1 lb) of purée add 375 g (12 oz) sugar. Heat gently, stirring from time to time, until the sugar has dissolved.

Cook over a medium heat for 45–60 minutes, stirring more frequently towards the end of cooking, until the mixture has darkened slightly and is so thick that the wooden spoon leaves a line across the base of the pan when drawn through the mixture. Skim with a draining spoon or stir in the butter if needed.

Ladle into warm, dry jars, filling to the very top. Clip on lids, label and leave to cool.

To serve, this makes a good accompaniment for cheese, crackers and grapes.

For plum & clove cheese, use 1.5 kg (3 lb) plums, count them, and add to the preserving pan with the cloves and 600 ml (1 pint) water. Cook as above, then remove the stones, making sure to count them to double-check that you have them all, before puréeing and continuing as above.

quince cheese

Makes **2 large jars**
Preparation time **45 minutes**
Cooking time **1¾–2 hours**

2 kg (4 lb) **quinces**, down
    rubbed off, rinsed, and cut
    into 2.5 cm (1 inch) cubes
2 litres (3½ pints) **water**
1.5–1.75 kg (3–3½ lb)
    granulated sugar
a little **sunflower oil**, for
    brushing the pan and the
    insides of the jars
15 g (½ oz) **butter** (optional)

Add the quinces to a large pan and pour over the measurement water. Cover and bring to the boil, then reduce the heat and simmer for 1 hour, until very soft.

Purée the quinces and their liquid in batches in a food processor or blender, then press through a sieve into a large bowl. Discard the seeds, skin and cores. Weigh the purée. Wash and dry the pan and brush with sunflower oil. Pour the purée back into the pan, add 500 g (1 lb) sugar for every 500 g (1 lb) purée, and cook over a low heat, stirring from time to time, until the sugar has dissolved.

Cook, uncovered, over a medium heat for 45–60 minutes, stirring more frequently towards the end of cooking, until the mixture makes large bubbles, has darkened slightly and it is so thick that the wooden spoon leaves a line across the base of the pan when drawn through the mixture. Skim with° a draining spoon or stir in the butter, if needed.

Ladle quickly into warm, wide-necked jars with tight-fitting lids (square if possible), the insides of which have been lightly brushed with sunflower oil, filling to the very top. Cover with screw-top lids, label and leave to cool.

To serve, loosen the quince cheese with a round-bladed knife, turn out and slice. Serve with bread and cheese.

For blackberry & apple cheese, quarter, core and peel 1.5 kg (3 lb) cooking apples, and cook with 500 g (1 lb) blackberries and 600 ml (1 pint) water for 30 minutes until soft. Purée, then weigh and add to the preserving pan with 375 g (12 oz) sugar for every 500 g (1 lb) of purée. Continue as above.

jellies

plum & crushed peppercorn jelly

Makes **7 jars**
Preparation time **25 minutes,
  plus straining**
Cooking time **40–50 minutes**

2 kg (4 lb) **plums**, left whole
1.2 litres (2 pints) **water**
about 1.25 kg (2½ lb)
  granulated sugar
2 teaspoons **multi-coloured
  peppercorns**, roughly
  crushed
2 teaspoons **pink
  peppercorns**, either dried or
  in brine, roughly crushed
15 g (½ oz) **butter** (optional)

Add the plums and measurement water to the preserving pan (there's no need to stone or slice the plums first). Bring to the boil, then cover and cook gently for 30 minutes, stirring and mashing the fruit from time to time with a fork, until soft.

Allow to cool slightly, then pour into a scalded jelly bag suspended over a large bowl and allow to drip for several hours.

Measure the clear liquid and pour back into the rinsed preserving pan. Weigh 500 g (1 lb) sugar for every 600 ml (1 pint) of liquid, then pour into the preserving pan. Add the peppercorns and heat gently, stirring from time to time, until the sugar has dissolved.

Bring to the boil, then boil rapidly until setting point is reached (10–20 minutes). Skim with a draining spoon or stir in butter if needed. Allow to stand for 5 minutes so that the peppercorns don't float to the surface.

Ladle into warm, dry jars, filling to the very top. Cover with screw-top lids, or with waxed discs and cellophane tops secured with elastic bands. Label and leave to cool.

To serve, this jelly works well with roast lamb and roast potatoes.

For plum & star anise jelly, add 7 small star anise instead of the peppercorns and make sure to include 1 per jar when potting.

gooseberry & rosemary jelly

Makes **4 assorted jars**
Preparation time **25 minutes,
  plus straining**
Cooking time **30–45 minutes**

1.5 kg (3 lb) **gooseberries,**
  no need to top and tail
1 litre (1¾ pints) **water**
4–5 stems **fresh rosemary**
about 875 g (1¾ lb)
  granulated sugar
15 g (½ oz) **butter** (optional)

Add the gooseberries, measurement water and rosemary to a preserving pan. Bring to the boil, then cover and simmer gently for 20–30 minutes, stirring and mashing the fruit from time to time with a fork, until soft.

Leave to cool slightly, then pour into a scalded jelly bag suspended over a large bowl and allow to drip for several hours.

Measure the clear liquid and pour back into the rinsed preserving pan. Weigh 500 g (1 lb) sugar for every 600 ml (1 pint) of liquid, then pour into the preserving pan. Heat gently, stirring from to time, until the sugar has dissolved.

Bring to the boil, then boil rapidly until setting point is reached (10–15 minutes). Skim with a draining spoon or stir in butter if needed.

Ladle into warm, dry jars, filling to the very top. Cover with screw-top lids, or with waxed discs and cellophane tops secured with elastic bands. Label and leave to cool.

To serve, try this jelly with grilled herrings and salad.

For sour apple & rosemary jelly, cook 1.5 kg (3 lb) cooking apples, roughly chopped (no need to peel or core first), with 750 ml (1¼ pints) water and 150 ml (¼ pint) white wine vinegar. Add rosemary and cook as above.

96

windfall apple & cider jelly

Makes **4 jars**
Preparation time **25 minutes,**
  plus straining
Cooking time **45–55 minutes**

2.5 kg (5 lb) **windfall apples**,
  weighed after cutting away
  any bruised areas
500 ml (17 fl oz) **dry cider**
900 ml (1 ½ pints) **water**
rind of **1 lemon**
about 1 kg (2 lb)
  granulated sugar
15 g (½ oz) **butter** (optional)

Wash and roughly chop the apples, without peeling or coring first. Add to a preserving pan with the cider, measurement water and lemon rind. Bring to the boil, then cover and simmer gently for 30 minutes, stirring and mashing the fruit from time to time with a fork, until soft.

Allow to cool slightly, then pour into a scalded jelly bag suspended over a large bowl and allow to drip for several hours.

Measure the clear liquid and pour back into the rinsed preserving pan. Weigh 500 g (1 lb) sugar for every 600 ml (1 pint) of liquid, then pour into the preserving pan. Heat gently, stirring from time to time, until the sugar has dissolved.

Bring to the boil, then boil rapidly until setting point is reached (15–25 minutes). Skim with a draining spoon or stir in butter if needed.

Ladle into warm, dry jars, filling to the very top. Cover with screw-top lids, or with waxed discs and cellophane tops secured with elastic bands. Label and leave to cool.

For windfall apple & ginger jelly, omit the cider and add 450 ml (¾ pint) of extra water. Cook, then drip as above. Add a 5 cm (2 inch) piece of root ginger, peeled and finely chopped, when adding the sugar. Continue as above.

bloody mary jelly

Makes **4 jars**
Preparation time **30 minutes,
  plus straining**
Cooking time **1 hour
  20 minutes–1 hour
  30 minutes**

250 g (8 oz) **red onions**,
  roughly chopped
125 g (4 oz) **sticks celery**,
  roughly chopped
1 kg (2 lb) **tomatoes**, roughly
  chopped (not skinned
  or deseeded)
500 g (1 lb) **windfall cooking
  apples**, any bruised areas
  cut away, roughly chopped
  (not peeled or cored)
600 ml (1 pint) **water**
200 ml (7 fl oz) **red wine
  vinegar**
about 1.25 kg (2½ lb)
  granulated sugar
1 tablespoon **tomato purée**
juice of 2 **lemons**
15 g (½ oz) **butter**, optional
50 g (2 oz) **sun-blush
  tomatoes** in oil, drained
  and diced
4 tablespoons **vodka**
  (optional)

Add the onions, celery, tomatoes and apples to a
preserving pan. Pour in the measurement water and
vinegar, then bring to the boil. Reduce the heat, cover
and simmer gently for 1 hour, stirring and mashing from
time to time with a fork, until the tomatoes and apples
are pulpy.

Allow to cool slightly, pour into a scalded jelly bag
suspended over a large bowl and allow to drip for
several hours.

Measure the clear liquid and then pour back into
the rinsed preserving pan. Weigh 500 g (1 lb) sugar
for every 600 ml (1 pint) of liquid, then pour into the
preserving pan. Add the tomato purée and lemon juice
and heat gently, stirring from time to time, until the
sugar has dissolved.

Bring to the boil, then boil rapidly until setting point is
reached (20–30 minutes).

Skim with a draining spoon or stir in butter if needed.
Stir in the sun-blush tomatoes and vodka, if liked, and
leave to stand for 15 minutes so that the tomatoes
don't rise in the jelly when potted. Ladle into warm, dry
jars, filling to the very top. Cover with screw-top lids,
or with waxed discs and cellophane tops secured with
elastic bands. Label and leave to cool.

To serve, this jelly goes well with cold meats, such as
salami and parma ham, olives and sunblush tomatoes.

For chilled tomato jelly, stir in 1 teaspoon dried
crushed red chillies with the tomato purée.

bitter lime & pernod jelly

Makes **3 small jars**
Preparation time **25 minutes,**
  plus straining
Cooking time **1 hour**
  5 minutes–1 hour
  10 minutes

6 large **limes** (about 500 g/
  1 lb in total) roughly chopped
500 g (1 lb) **pears**, roughly
  chopped (no need to peel
  and core)
1.2 litres (2 pints) **water**
about 750 g (1½ lb)
  granulated sugar
6 tablespoons **Pernod**
15 g (½ oz) **butter** (optional)

Add the limes, pears and measurement water to a preserving pan, bring to the boil, then cover and cook gently for 1 hour, stirring and mashing the fruit from time to time with a fork, until soft.

Allow to cool slightly, then pour into a scalded jelly bag suspended over a large bowl and allow to drip for several hours.

Measure the clear liquid and pour back into the rinsed preserving pan. Weigh 500 g (1 lb) sugar for every 600 ml (1 pint) of liquid, then pour into the preserving pan. Add the Pernod and cook gently, stirring from time to time, until the sugar has dissolved.

Bring to the boil, then boil rapidly until setting point is reached (5–10 minutes). Skim with a draining spoon or stir in butter if needed.

Ladle into warm, dry jars, filling to the very top. Cover with screw-top lids, or with waxed discs and cellophane tops secured with elastic bands. Label and leave to cool.

To serve, try spreading baguette slices with cream cheese, then top with smoked salmon, jelly and watercress.

For bitter lemon & lime jelly, replace the limes with a mixture of lemons and limes, then continue as above, omitting the Pernod.

rosehip & apple jelly

Makes **4 assorted jars**
Preparation time **30 minutes,
    plus straining**
Cooking time **55 minutes–
    1¼ hours**

400 g (13 oz) ripe **red
    rosehips**, left whole
1 kg (2 lb) **cooking apples**,
    roughly chopped (no need
    to peel or core)
1 litre (1¾ pints) **water**
about 875 g (1¾ lb)
    granulated sugar
juice of **1 lemon**
15 g (½ oz) **butter** (optional)

Add the hips and apples to a preserving pan with the measurement water. Bring to the boil, then cover and simmer gently for 45–60 minutes, stirring and mashing the fruit from time to time with a fork, until soft.

Leave to cool slightly, then pour into a scalded jelly bag suspended over a large bowl and allow to drip for several hours.

Measure the clear liquid and pour back into the rinsed preserving pan. Weigh 500 g (1 lb) sugar for every 600 ml (1 pint) of liquid, then pour into the preserving pan. Add the lemon juice and heat gently, stirring from time to time, until the sugar has dissolved.

Bring to the boil, then boil rapidly until setting point is reached (10–15 minutes). Skim with a draining spoon or stir in butter if needed.

Ladle into warm, dry jars, filling to the very top. Cover with screw-top lids, or with waxed discs and cellophane tops secured with elastic bands. Label and leave to cool.

For elderberry & apple jelly, make up the jelly with 750 g (1½ lb) elderberries, stripped from their stems, and 750 g (1½ lb) cooking apples, roughly chopped but not peeled or cored, and cook in 900 ml (1½ pints) water for about 40 minutes until the fruit is soft. Continue as above.

minted blackberry & apple jelly

Makes **6 jars**
Preparation time **25 minutes,**
 plus straining
Cooking time **40 minutes–**
 1 hour

2 kg (4 lb) **cooking apples,**
 roughly chopped (no need
 to peel or core)
500 g (1 lb) **blackberries**
1.2 litres (2 pints) **water**
1.5 kg (3 lb) g**ranulated sugar**
15 g (½ oz) **butter** (optional)
20 g (¾ oz) fresh **mint,**
 finely chopped

Add the apples, blackberries and measurement water
to a preserving pan, bring to the boil, then cover and
cook gently for 30–40 minutes, stirring and mashing
the fruit from time to time with a fork, until soft.

Leave to cool slightly, then pour into a scalded jelly
bag suspended over a large bowl and allow to drip for
several hours.

Measure the clear liquid and pour back into the rinsed
preserving pan. Weigh 500 g (1 lb) sugar for every
600 ml (1 pint) of liquid, then pour into the preserving
pan. Heat gently, stirring from time to time, until the
sugar has dissolved.

Bring to the boil, then boil rapidly until setting point
is reached (10–20 minutes). Skim with a draining
spoon or stir in butter if needed. Leave to cool for
5–10 minutes, then stir in the mint.

Ladle into warm, dry jars. If the mint begins to float,
leave to cool for 5–10 minutes more, then stir very
gently with a teaspoon to redistribute the mint. Cover
with screw-top lids, or with waxed discs and cellophane
tops secured with elastic bands. Label and leave to cool.

To serve, this jelly is a great accompaniment for drop
scones and butter.

For quince, apple & cinnamon jelly, roughly chop
1.25 kg (2½ lb) cooking apples and 1.25 kg (2½ lb)
quinces, then add to the preserving pan with a 7.5 cm
(3 inch) piece cinnamon stick, broken in half, and
1.2 litres (2 pints) water. Cover and cook gently as
above, then strain and boil with sugar as above.

redcurrant & lavender jelly

Makes **6 small jars**
Preparation time **25 minutes,**
  plus straining
Cooking time **30–40 minutes**

1.5 kg (3 lb) **redcurrants**
1 litre (1¾ pints) **water**
about 1 kg (2 lb)
  granulated sugar
15 g (½ oz) **butter** (optional)
8–10 **dried lavender heads**

Strip the redcurrants from their stalks with a fork and add to a preserving pan with the measurement water. Bring to the boil, then cover and simmer gently for 20 minutes, stirring and mashing the fruit from time to time with a fork, until soft.

Leave to cool slightly, then pour into a scalded jelly bag suspended over a large bowl and allow to drip for several hours.

Measure the clear liquid and pour back into the rinsed preserving pan. Weigh 500 g (1 lb) sugar for every 600 ml (1 pint) of liquid, then pour into the preserving pan. Heat gently, stirring from time to time, until the sugar has dissolved.

Bring to the boil, then boil rapidly until setting point is reached (10–20 minutes). Skim with a draining spoon or stir in butter if needed. Leave to cool for 5–10 minutes.

Ladle into warm, dry jars, filling to the very top. Cover with screw-top lids, or with waxed discs and cellophane tops secured with elastic bands. Label and leave to cool.

To serve, pair with scones or spoon onto a cream-topped pavlova with extra strawberries.

For redcurrant & orange jelly, reduce the amount of water to 900 ml (1½ pints) when cooking the redcurrants, then add the juice of 2 oranges when measuring out the juice at the end. Omit the lavender flowers.

strawberry & rhubarb jelly

Makes **4 jars**

Preparation time **25 minutes, plus straining**

Cooking time **50–60 minutes**

1 kg (2 lb) **strawberries**, halved if large

500 g (1 lb) **trimmed rhubarb**, thickly sliced

1 litre (1¾ pints) **water**

about 875 g (1¾ lb) **granulated sugar**

juice of 2 **lemons**

15 g (½ oz) **butter** (optional)

Add the strawberries and rhubarb to a preserving pan, pour over the measurement water to just cover the fruit, then bring to the boil. Cover and simmer gently for 30 minutes, stirring and mashing the fruit from time to time with a fork, until soft.

Allow to cool slightly, then pour into a scalded jelly bag suspended over a large bowl and allow to drip for several hours.

Measure the clear liquid and then pour back into the rinsed preserving pan. Weigh 500 g (1 lb) sugar for every 600 ml (1 pint) of liquid, then pour into the preserving pan. Add the lemon juice, heat gently, stirring from time to time, until the sugar has dissolved.

Bring to the boil, then boil rapidly until setting point is reached (20–30 minutes). Skim with a draining spoon or stir in butter if needed.

Ladle into warm, dry jars. Cover with screw-top lids, or with waxed discs and cellophane tops secured with elastic bands. Label and leave to cool.

To serve, this jelly makes a lovely filling for a Swiss roll.

For mulberry & apple jelly, cook 500 g (1 lb) roughly chopped cooking apples in 300 ml (½ pint) water in a covered preserving pan for 10 minutes until just beginning to soften. Add 1 kg (2 lb) mulberries and cook for 20 minutes, stirring and crushing from time to time, until soft. Strain and continue as above.

grape & port jelly

Makes **3–4 jars**
Preparation time **10 minutes,**
  plus straining
Cooking time **1 hour**
  10 minutes–1 hour
  15 minutes

1 kg (2 lb) **red grapes with**
  stalks, halved
3 **lemons**, halved
1.8 litres (3 pints) **water**
about 750 g (1½ lb)
  granulated sugar
150 ml (¼ pint) **port**
15 g (½ oz) **butter** (optional)

Add the grapes and their stalks to a large preserving
pan. Squeeze and reserve the juice from the lemons.
Chop the lemon shells and add to the pan with the
measurement water. Bring to the boil, reduce the heat
and cover the pan. Simmer for 1 hour.

Allow to cool, then pour into a scolded jelly bag
suspended over a large bowl and allow to drip for
several hours or overnight.

Measure the clear liquid and pour back into the rinsed
preserving pan. Weigh 375 g (12 oz) sugar for every
600 ml (1 pint) of liquid, then pour into the preserving
pan. Pour in the port and reserved lemon juice and cook
over a low heat, stirring continuously, until the sugar has
dissolved. Bring to the boil, then boil rapidly until setting
point is reached (10–15 minutes). Skim with a draining
spoon or stir in butter, if needed.

Ladle into warm, dry jars. Cover with screw-top lids,
or with waxed discs and cellophane tops secured with
elastic bands. Label and leave to cool.

To serve drizzle the jelly over vanilla ice cream.

For crab apple jelly, roughly chop 2 kg (4 lb) crab apples
and add to a preserving pan with 1.2 litres (2 pints) water,
the juice of 2 lemons and 4 cloves. Cover and simmer for
1½ hours, strain, then add 375 g (12 oz) granulated sugar
for each 600 ml (1 pint) of juice. Continue as above.

marmalades

dark oxford marmalade

Makes **5–6 jars**
Preparation time **30 minutes**
Cooking time **1 hour**
   40 minutes–1 hour
   50 minutes

1 kg (2 lb) Seville or regular
   oranges (about 6)
1.8 litres (3 pints) **water**
juice of 1 **lemon**
1.75 kg (3½ lb) **granulated**
   sugar, warmed
250 g (8 oz) **dark muscovado**
   sugar, warmed
15 g (½ oz) **butter** (optional)

Cut each orange into 6 wedges, then thinly slice. Tie the orange pips in a square of muslin. Add oranges and pips to a preserving pan, pour over the measurement water and add the lemon juice. Bring slowly to the boil, then simmer gently, uncovered, for about 1½ hours until reduced by almost half.

Add the sugar and heat gently, stirring occasionally, until dissolved. Bring to the boil, then boil rapidly until setting point is reached (10–20 minutes).

Lift out the muslin bag, squeezing well. Skim with a draining spoon or stir in butter if needed. Ladle into warm, dry jars, filling to the very top. Cover with screw-top lids, or with waxed discs and cellophane tops secured with elastic bands. Label and leave to cool.

To serve, this marmalade goes beautifully with sliced walnut bread.

For golden Oxford marmalade, omit the dark muscovado sugar and use 2 kg (4 lb) granulated sugar in place of the amount used in the main recipe.

apple & orange marmalade

Makes **10 jars**
Preparation time **30 minutes**
Cooking time **1 hour**
  50 minutes–2½ hours

750 g (1½ lb) **oranges**
  (about 4–5)
2 **lemons**
1.2–1.5 litres (2–2½ pints)
  water
1 kg (2 lb) **windfall apples**,
  weighed after any bruised
  areas are cut away
1.75 kg (3½ lb) **granulated
  sugar**
15 g (½ oz) **butter**

Chop the oranges and lemons, then add to a preserving pan. Tie the pips in a square of muslin and add to the pan. Pour in 1 litre (1¾ pints) water, bring to the boil, then cover and simmer for 1½–2 hours. Stir now and then and check that the fruit doesn't boil dry. Top up with a little extra water if needed. Meanwhile, peel, quarter and core the apples. Chop, then add to a saucepan with 150 ml (¼ pint) water. Cover and cook gently for 20 minutes, stirring now and then, until soft.

Leave the citrus fruits and apple to cool. Lift out the muslin bag, squeezing well. Blend the citrus fruit and apples together in small batches in a food processor or liquidizer, adding the remaining water as needed to aid blending.

Pour the fruit into the preserving pan, add the sugar, then heat gently, stirring now and then until the sugar has dissolved. Bring to the boil, then boil rapidly until setting point is reached (20–30 minutes). Skim with a draining spoon or stir in butter, if needed.

Ladle into warm, dry jars, filling to the very top. Cover with screw-top lids, or with waxed discs and cellophane tops secured with elastic bands. Label and leave to cool.

To serve, try it with hot buttered English muffins.

For chunky fig, almond & orange marmalade, slice the oranges and lemons, then cook in 1 litre (1¾ pints) water for 1½–2 hours or until soft. Cook 500 g (1 lb) dried chopped figs in 300 ml (½ pint) water, covered, for 20 minutes until soft. Stir the figs into the softened citrus fruit and purée together, then add to the preserving pan with 50 g (2 oz) roughly chopped blanched almonds and 1.75 kg (3½ lb) granulated sugar, and continue as above.

apricot, orange & ginger marmalade

Makes **5 jars**

Preparation time **25 minutes, plus soaking**

Cooking time **1 hour–1 hour 5 minutes**

500 g (1 lb) **oranges** (about 3)

1 **lemon**

250 g (8 oz) **ready-to-eat dried apricots**

5 cm (2 inch) **piece root ginger**, peeled

1.2 litres (2 pints) **water**

1.5 kg (3 lb) **granulated sugar**, warmed

15 g (½ oz) **butter** (optional)

Halve the oranges and lemon and squeeze out the juice into a bowl. Scrape out the pith and pips and tie in a muslin bag.

Cut the fruit shells into very thin slices. Dice the apricots and finely chop the ginger. Add to the fruit juice and mix in the measurement water, then add the muslin bag. Cover the bowl and leave to soak overnight in a cool place.

Pour the fruit mix into a preserving pan, cover and cook gently for 45 minutes until tender. Add the sugar and heat gently, stirring from time to time, until dissolved.

Bring to the boil, then boil rapidly until setting point is reached (15–20 minutes). Lift out the muslin bag, squeezing well. Skim with a draining spoon or add the butter if needed.

Allow to cool for 10 minutes, then ladle into warm, dry jars, filling to the very top. Cover with screw-top lids, or with waxed discs and cellophane tops secured with elastic bands. Label and leave to cool.

To serve, this marmalade makes a good topping for a steamed pudding made with light muscovado sugar and ginger.

For apricot, orange & cardamom marmalade, omit the ginger and add 10 cardamom pods that have been split, adding the pods and seeds to the sliced fruit rinds and diced apricots. Continue as above.

lime jelly marmalade

Makes **4 jars**
Preparation time **30 minutes,
  plus straining**
Cooking time **1 hour
  20 minutes–1 hour
  30 minutes**

750 g (1½ lb) **limes** (about 10)
500 g (1 lb) **lemons** (about 6)
1.8 litres (3 pints) **water**
1.25 kg (2½ lb) **granulated
  sugar**
15 g (½ oz) **butter** (optional)

Pare the rind from the limes and lemons with a vegetable peeler, then cut into very fine shreds and set aside. Roughly chop the peeled fruits and put into a preserving pan with 1.2 litres (2 pints) water. Cover and cook gently for 1 hour or until soft.

Meanwhile, add the fruit rinds to a saucepan with the remaining water, bring to the boil, reduce the heat to a simmer and cook, covered, for 20 minutes, until softened.

Pour the contents of the preserving pan through a fine sieve or jelly bag suspended over a large bowl. Leave to drip for several hours, then squeeze the bag to extract as much juice as possible.

Return the strained juice to the preserving pan with the cooked fruit rinds and their cooking liquid. Add the sugar and heat gently, stirring from time to time, until completely dissolved. Bring to the boil, then boil rapidly until setting point is reached (20–30 minutes).

Skim with a draining spoon or stir in butter if needed. Leave to stand for 10 minutes so that the fruit rinds will not rise in the jelly when potted.

Ladle into warm, dry jars, filling to the very top. Cover with screw-top lids, or with waxed discs and cellophane tops secured with elastic bands. Label and leave to cool.

For ginger & lemon jelly marmalade, omit the limes, then prepare and cook 1.25 kg (2½ lb) lemons as above. Cook the lemon rind shreds in the remaining water with a 7.5 cm (3 inch) piece of root ginger that has been peeled and finely chopped for 20 minutes. Strain the marmalade base and continue as above.

grapefruit jelly marmalade

Makes **3 jars**
Preparation time **30 minutes,
  plus straining**
Cooking time **1 hour
  10 minutes–1 hour
  20 minutes**

1.25 kg (2½ lb) **pink
  grapefruits** (about 4)
1.8 litres (3 pints) **water**
1 kg (2 lb) **granulated sugar**
15 g (½ oz) **butter** (optional)

Peel the grapefruits with a vegetable peeler, then cut the rind into very fine shreds and set aside. Roughly chop the peeled fruits and put into a preserving pan with 1.2 litres (2 pints) water. Cover and cook gently for 1 hour or until soft.

Meanwhile, add the fruit rinds to a saucepan, pour over the remaining water, bring to the boil, then cover and simmer gently for 20 minutes or until tender.

Pour the contents of the preserving pan through a fine sieve or jelly bag suspended over a large bowl. Leave to drip for several hours, then squeeze the bag to extract as much juice as possible.

Return the strained juice to the preserving pan with the cooked fruit rinds and their cooking liquid. Reheat, then add the sugar and heat gently, stirring from time to time, until the sugar has completely dissolved.

Bring to the boil, then boil rapidly until setting point is reached (10–20 minutes). Skim with a draining spoon or stir in butter if needed. Leave to cool for 10 minutes so that the fruit rinds will not rise in the jelly when potted.

Ladle into warm, dry jars, filling to the very top. Cover with screw-top lids, or with waxed discs and cellophane tops secured with elastic bands. Label and leave to cool.

To serve, try this marmalade with buttered brioche and lemon tea.

For ruby orange marmalade, make up the marmalade as above with 1.25 kg (2½ lb) mixed red-fleshed grapefruit and blood oranges, mixed half and half. Continue as above.

lemon & quince marmalade

Makes **4 jars**
Preparation time **30 minutes,
  plus straining**
Cooking time **40–50 minutes**

500 g (1 lb) **lemons** (about 5)
1.5 kg (3 lb) **quinces**
1.5 litres (2½ pints) **water**
1.5 kg (3 lb) **granulated sugar**
15 g (½ oz) **butter** (optional)

Peel the lemons with a vegetable peeler, then cut the rind into fine shreds and set aside. Squeeze the juice into a bowl. Reserve the pips, then roughly chop the lemon shells.

Peel one quarter of the quinces, halve and core. Cut the flesh into thin strips and add to the lemon juice so that they don't discolour. Add the quince peelings, core and quince seeds to a preserving pan. Roughly chop the remaining unpeeled quinces, add to the preserving pan with the lemon shells and reserved pips.

Add 1 litre (1¾ pints) water to the preserving pan, cover and cook gently for 30 minutes or until the quinces are soft. Pour through a jelly bag suspended over a bowl and leave to drip for 30 minutes or until cool enough to squeeze the bag to extract as much juice as possible. You should have about 600 ml (1 pint) of juice. Meanwhile, add the lemon rind, sliced quince, lemon juice and remaining water to a small saucepan and cook, covered, for 20 minutes, until just tender.

Pour the squeezed quince juice back into the preserving pan, add the lemon rind, sliced quince and cooking water. Pour in the sugar and heat gently, stirring from time to time, until dissolved. Increase the heat and boil rapidly until setting point is reached (10–20 minutes).

Skim with a draining spoon or stir in butter if needed. Leave to stand for 10 minutes, then ladle into warm, dry jars, filling to the very top. Cover with screw-top lids, or with waxed discs and cellophane tops secured with elastic bands. Label and leave to cool.

For lemon & pear marmalade, make as above using 1.5 kg (3 lb) firm pears instead of quinces.

pineapple marmalade

Makes **3 jars**
Preparation time **30 minutes**
Cooking time **50–60 minutes**

1 large **pineapple**, trimmed,
   peeled, quartered and cored
2 **stems lemon grass**
grated rind of **4 limes**
125 ml (4 fl oz) freshly
   squeezed **lime juice**,
   (about 3–4 limes)
450 ml (¾ pint) **chilled
   pineapple juice** (from
   a carton)
750 g (1½ lb) **granulated
   sugar**
15 g (½ oz) **butter** (optional)

Finely chop three quarters of the pineapple in a food processor or using a knife. Cut the remaining pineapple into small cubes. Slit the lemon grass stems and bruise with a rolling pin, then tie the stems together in the centre with string.

Add the pineapple and lemon grass to a preserving pan, then add the lime rind and juice and the pineapple juice. Bring to the boil, cover and simmer gently for 30 minutes.

Pour in the sugar and heat gently, stirring from time to time, until the sugar has dissolved. Bring to the boil, then boil rapidly until setting point is reached (20–30 minutes). Remove the lemon grass. Skim with a draining spoon or stir in butter if needed.

Ladle into warm, dry jars, filling to the very top. Cover with screw-top lids, or with waxed discs and cellophane tops secured with elastic bands. Label and leave to cool.

For pineapple, mango & lime marmalade, make up using ½ large trimmed, peeled, quartered and cored pineapple, 2 medium mangoes, stoned, peeled and diced, and the lime rind and juice as above, but omit the lemon grass. Cook in the pineapple juice, then continue as above.

pressure cooker marmalade

Makes **4 assorted jars**
Preparation time **30 minutes**
Cooking time **20–30 minutes**

750 g (1½ lb) **oranges**
  (about 4 medium ones)
juice of 2 l**emons**
600 ml (1 pint) **water**
1.25 kg (2½ lb) **granulated**
  sugar
15 g (½ oz) **butter**

Halve the oranges and squeeze the juice. Quarter, then scrape away the membrane and pith, leaving a thin layer of pith still attached to the rind. Tie the membrane, pith and pips in a square of muslin. Thinly slice the orange rind.

Remove the trivet from the base of the pressure cooker. Add the shredded orange rind, orange juice, lemon juice and muslin bag to the pressure cooker, then pour on the measurement water. Cover with the pressure cooker lid, bring up to medium pressure, then reduce the heat slightly so that the pressure cooker gently hisses and indicates that the correct pressure has been reached. Cook for 10 minutes, then leave to cool and allow the pressure to release slowly.

Remove the pressure cooker lid. Lift the muslin bag a little above the contents of the pressure cooker and press between two wooden spoons to remove as much pectin-rich juice as possible, then discard the bag. Check that the rind is just tender – if not, bring back to pressure and cook for a further 2–3 minutes.

Pour in the sugar and heat gently, without the lid, until the sugar has dissolved, stirring from time to time. Bring to the boil, then boil rapidly until setting point is reached (10–20 minutes). Skim with a draining spoon or stir in butter if needed. Allow to stand for 10 minutes.

Ladle into warm, dry jars, filling to the very top. Cover with screw-top lids, or with waxed discs and cellophane tops secured with elastic bands. Label and leave to cool.

For orange & lime marmalade, replace the oranges with 750 g (1½ lb) mixed oranges and limes. Continue as above.

mixed citrus marmalade

Makes **4 jars**
Preparation time **30 minutes**
Cooking time **1 hour
10 minutes–1 hour
20 minutes**

2 **oranges**
2 **lemons**
2 **limes**
1 **red-fleshed grapefruit**
1 **pink-fleshed grapefruit**
1.8 litres (3 pints) **water**
1.25 kg (2½ lb) **granulated
sugar**, warmed
15 g (½ oz) **butter** (optional)

Peel the fruits with a vegetable peeler, then cut the rind into very fine shreds. Add to a saucepan with 600 ml (1 pint) water, bring to the boil, then cover and simmer gently for 20 minutes until the rinds are tender.

Meanwhile, roughly chop the peeled fruits, put into a preserving pan with 1.2 litres (2 pints) water, cover and simmer gently for 1 hour until soft.

Strain the fruit mixture through a fine nylon sieve or jelly bag into a large bowl, pressing the pulp to extract all the juice. Return to the preserving pan, stir in the cooked fruit rinds and cooking water and reheat.

Add the sugar and heat gently, stirring from time to time, until the sugar has dissolved. Bring to the boil, then boil rapidly until setting point is reached (10–20 minutes). Skim with a draining spoon or stir in butter if needed.

Leave to cool for 10 minutes, then ladle into warm, dry jars, filling to the very top. Cover with screw-top lids, or with waxed discs and cellophane tops secured with elastic bands. Label and leave to cool.

To serve, try spreading this marmalade over a lemon tart.

For three-fruit shred marmalade, omit the grapefruit and add 1.25 kg (2½ lb) mixed oranges, lemons and limes, then continue as above.

chutneys

mango & pineapple chutney

Makes **3 jars**
Preparation time **30 minutes**
Cooking time **20 minutes**

300 ml (½ pint) **distilled malt vinegar**
375 g (12 oz) **granulated sugar**
2 **garlic cloves**, finely chopped
5 cm (2 inch) piece **root ginger**, peeled and finely chopped
4 **dried chillies**, finely chopped
½ teaspoon **ground allspice**
1 teaspoon **salt**
1 teaspoon mixed **peppercorns**, roughly crushed
1 large **pineapple**, trimmed, peeled, cored and finely chopped in a food processor
2 large, firm, **unripe mangoes**, peeled, stoned and sliced

Add the vinegar, sugar, garlic and ginger to a preserving pan, then add the dried chillies, allspice, salt and peppercorns. Heat gently, stirring from time to time, until the sugar has dissolved, then simmer gently for 10 minutes so that the flavours mingle together.

Stir in the pineapple and sliced mango and cook over a medium heat for 10 minutes until the mango is just translucent and the liquid is syrupy.

Ladle into warm, dry jars, filling to the very top. Press the mango slices beneath the syrup, then cover with screw-top lids. Label and leave to mature in a cool, dark place for at least 3 weeks.

To serve, partner with poppadums.

For mango & black onion seed chutney, make as above, omitting the pineapple. Peel and stone 4 large, firm, unripe mangoes, finely chop 2 of them and slice the remaining 2. Continue as above, adding 2 tablespoons black onion seeds.

garlicky mediterranean chutney

Makes **3 jars**
Preparation time **20 minutes**
Cooking time **1½ hours**

1 **garlic bulb** (about 12 cloves),
    peeled and finely chopped
300 g (10 oz) **onions**,
    chopped
500 g (1 lb) **tomatoes**,
    skinned (optional) and
    roughly chopped
500 g (1 lb) **courgettes**, diced
6 **peppers** of different colours,
    halved, deseeded and cut
    into strips
250 ml (8 fl oz) **red wine**
    vinegar
250 g (8 oz) **granulated**
    sugar
1 tablespoon **tomato purée**
3 stems **rosemary**, leaves
    chopped
salt and **pepper**

Add all the ingredients to a preserving pan and cook, uncovered, over a gentle heat for 1½ hours, stirring from time to time, but more frequently towards the end of cooking as the chutney thickens.

Ladle into warm, dry jars, filling to the very top and pressing down well. Disperse any air pockets with a skewer or small knife and cover with screw-top lids. Label and leave to mature in a cool, dark place for at least 3 weeks.

For ratatouille chutney, reduce the garlic to 4 cloves, add 375 g (12 oz) diced courgettes, 4 peppers, cored, deseeded and diced, and 1 aubergine, diced. Mix with the onions, tomatoes, vinegar, sugar, rosemary and tomato purée and continue as above.

aubergine & mint chutney

Makes **4 jars**
Preparation time **30 minutes**
Cooking time **1½–1¾ hours**

1 kg (2 lb) **aubergines** (about
    4 medium ones), diced
300 g (10 oz) **red onions**
    (about 3), chopped
500 g (1 lb) **tomatoes**,
    skinned (optional) and
    roughly chopped
4 cloves **garlic**, finely chopped
200 g (7 oz) **stoned dates**,
    diced
300 ml (½ pint) **red wine
    vinegar**
250 g (8 oz) **light muscovado
    sugar**
2 teaspoons **coriander seeds**,
    roughly crushed
2 teaspoons **cumin seeds**,
    roughly crushed
1 teaspoon **paprika**
1 teaspoon **salt**
4 tablespoons **chopped mint**

Add all the ingredients except the mint to a preserving pan, cover and cook over a gentle heat for 1 hour, stirring from time to time, until softened. Remove the lid and cook for 30–45 minutes until thick, stirring more frequently towards the end of cooking as the chutney thickens. Stir the mint into the chutney.

Ladle into warm, dry jars, filling to the very top and pressing down well. Disperse any air pockets with a skewer or small knife and cover with screw-top lids. Label and leave to mature in a cool, dark place for at least 3 weeks.

To serve, this chutney is delicious as a mezze starter with olives, marinated peppers, yogurt mixed with chopped mint, and griddled pitta bread.

For aubergine & chilli chutney, add 1–2 large mild red chillies, to taste, finely chopped and seeds discarded, when adding the garlic. Stir 4 tablespoons chopped coriander into the cooked chutney instead of the mint.

ale, apple & mustard chutney

Makes **4 jars**
Preparation time **30 minutes**
Cooking time **1¾–2 hours**

1 kg (2 lb) **cooking apples**,
  quartered, cored, peeled
  and diced
500 g (1 lb) **onions**, finely
  chopped
250 g (8 oz) **celery**, diced
250 g (8 oz) ready diced
  stoned dates
550 ml bottle **brown ale**
150 ml (¼ pint) **malt vinegar**
300 g (10 oz) **demerara
  sugar**
2 tablespoons **white mustard**
  seeds, roughly crushed
1 teaspoon **turmeric**
1 teaspoon **salt**
1 teaspoon **peppercorns**,
  roughly crushed

Add all the ingredients to a preserving pan and cook, uncovered, over a gentle heat for 1¾–2 hours, stirring from time to time, but more frequently towards the end of cooking as the chutney thickens.

Ladle into warm, dry jars, filling to the very top and pressing down well. Disperse any air pockets with a skewer or small knife and cover with screw-top lids. Label and leave to mature in a cool, dark place for at least 3 weeks.

To serve, this chutney is delicious as part of a ploughman's lunch.

For apple & ginger beer chutney, replace the ale with ginger beer and add sultanas in place of the dates. Continue and cook as above.

autumn harvest chutney

Makes **6 jars**
Preparation time **30 minutes**
Cooking time **1½ hours**

1 kg (2 lb) mixed **green** and
  red tomatoes, roughly
  chopped
500 g (1 lb) **red plums**,
  stoned and roughly chopped
1 **marrow** (about 750 g/
  1½ lb), peeled, halved,
  deseeded and diced
500 g (1 lb) **onions**, roughly
  chopped
100 g (3½ oz) **sultanas** or
  raisins
300 ml (½ pint) **distilled malt
  vinegar**
250 g (8 oz) **granulated
  sugar**
1 tablespoon **tomato purée**
2 teaspoons **hot paprika**
2 teaspoons **English mustard
  powder**
1 teaspoon **salt**
2 teaspoons **peppercorns**,
  roughly crushed

Add all the ingredients to a preserving pan, stir to
combine, then cook, uncovered, over a gentle heat for
1½ hours, stirring from time to time, but more frequently
towards the end of cooking as the chutney thickens.

Ladle into warm, dry jars, filling to the very top and
pressing down well. Disperse any air pockets with a
skewer or small knife and cover with screw-top lids.
Label and leave to mature in a cool, dark place for at
least 3 weeks.

For apple & tomato chutney, omit the plums and add
500 g (1 lb) peeled, cored and diced cooking apples.

runner bean chutney

Makes **6 jars**
Preparation time **25 minutes**
Cooking time **about
35 minutes**

1 kg (2 lb) **runner beans**,
  trimmed
900 ml (1½ pints) **distilled
  malt vinegar**
750 g (1½ lb) **demerara
  sugar**
500 g (1 lb) **onions**, chopped
1½ tablespoons **turmeric**
1½ tablespoons **mustard
  powder**
3 tablespoons **black
  mustard seeds**
3 tablespoons **cornflour**
1 teaspoon **salt**
pepper
3 tablespoons **water**

Half-fill a preserving pan with water, bring to the boil, then add the runner beans. Return to the boil and cook for 3 minutes. Drain into a colander, refresh with cold water, then drain again. Thinly slice the beans or roughly chop in a food processor.

Add the vinegar and sugar to the drained preserving pan, then add the onions. Cover and bring to the boil, then reduce the heat and simmer for 10 minutes.

Mix the remaining dry ingredients together in a bowl, then stir in the measurement water until smooth. Stir this into the vinegar mixture, then simmer, uncovered, for 10 minutes, stirring until smooth and thickened.

Stir the blanched beans into the vinegar mixture and cook gently for 10 minutes, stirring frequently until just tender. Ladle into warm, dry jars, pressing the beans down well in the vinegar mix. Disperse any air pockets with a skewer or small knife and cover with screw-top lids. Label and leave to mature in a cool, dark place for at least 3 weeks.

For courgette & mixed bean chutney, blanch 750 g (1½ lb) mixed green, black and yellow French beans with a few runner beans as above, then drain and chop. Add to the cooked vinegar and onion mixture with 250 g (8 oz) diced courgettes. Continue as above.

green tomato chutney

Makes **4 jars**
Preparation time **15 minutes**
Cooking time **1¼–1½ hours**

1 kg (2 lb) **green tomatoes**,
  finely chopped
500 g (1 lb) **onions**, finely
  chopped
500 g (1 lb) **cooking apples**,
  peeled, cored and chopped
2 **fresh green chillies**,
  halved, deseeded and
  finely chopped
2 **garlic cloves**, crushed
1 teaspoon **ground ginger**
generous pinch of **ground
  cloves**
generous pinch of **ground
  turmeric**
50 g (2 oz) **raisins**
250 g (8 oz) **soft dark brown
  sugar**
300 ml (½ pint) **white wine
  vinegar**

Add the tomatoes, onions, apples and chillies to a large
pan and mix together. Add the garlic, ginger, cloves and
turmeric, then stir in the raisins, sugar and vinegar.

Bring to the boil, then reduce the heat and simmer,
covered, for 1¼–1½ hours, or until the chutney has
thickened, stirring frequently.

Ladle into warm, dry jars. Disperse any air pockets with
a skewer or small knife and cover with screw-top lids.
Label and leave to mature in a cool, dark place for at
least 3 weeks.

For green tomato & mango chutney, peel 1 large,
ripe mango and cut the flesh from the stone. Dice the
flesh and add this in place of the apples to the green
tomatoes and onions. Add the chillies, spices and
100 g (3½ oz) ready-to-eat dried chopped apricots
with the sugar and vinegar. Cook as above.

pumpkin & walnut chutney

Makes **4 jars**
Preparation time **30 minutes**
Cooking time **1½–2 hours**

1 kg (2 lb) **pumpkin**, weighed
    after peeling and deseeding
2 **onions**, finely chopped
1 large **orange**, finely chopped,
    including skin and pith
600 ml (1 pint) **white wine**
    vinegar
375 g (12 oz) **granulated**
    sugar
1 **cinnamon stick**, halved
5 cm (2 inch) piece **root**
    ginger, peeled and finely
    chopped
1 teaspoon **turmeric**
1 teaspoon **dried crushed**
    red chillies
1 teaspoon **salt**
a little **pepper**
50 g (2 oz) **walnut pieces**

Dice the pumpkin, then add to a preserving pan with all the remaining ingredients. Cover and cook gently for 1 hour, stirring from time to time, until softened. Remove the lid and cook for ½–1 hour, stirring more frequently towards the end of cooking as the chutney thickens.

Ladle into warm, dry jars, filling to the very top and pressing down well. Disperse any air pockets with a skewer or small knife and cover with screw-top lids. Label and leave to mature in a cool, dark place for at least 3 weeks.

For pumpkin & date chutney, omit the walnut pieces and add 125 g (4 oz) ready-diced stoned dates instead.

pumpkin & red pepper chutney

Makes **3 jars**
Preparation time **30 minutes**
Cooking time **1¼ hours**

1 kg (2 lb) **pumpkin**, weighed
  after peeling and deseeding,
  sliced
2 **red peppers**, quartered,
  deseeded and cored
500 g (1 lb) **shallots**, peeled,
  halved if large
3 **bay leaves**
3 tablespoons **olive oil**
400 ml (14 fl oz) **cider** or
  white wine vinegar
125 g (4 oz) **granulated
  sugar**
125 g (4 oz) **light muscovado
  sugar**
1 teaspoon **allspice berries**,
  roughly crushed
½ teaspoon **salt**
½ teaspoon **cayenne pepper**

Add the pumpkin, red peppers and shallots to a large roasting tin. Tuck the bay leaves in among the vegetables, then drizzle with the oil. Roast in a preheated oven, 200°C (400°F), Gas Mark 6, for 45 minutes until the vegetables are tender and browned.

Leave to cool slightly, then remove the skins from the peppers. Roughly chop the peppers, pumpkin and shallots, discarding the bay leaves. Add the vegetables and any juices from the roasting to a preserving pan. Add all the remaining ingredients, then bring to the boil and simmer, uncovered, for about 30 minutes, stirring more frequently towards the end of cooking, until thick.

Ladle into warm, dry jars, filling to the very top and pressing down well. Disperse any air pockets with a skewer or small knife and cover with screw-top lids. Label and leave to mature in a cool, dark place for at least 3 weeks.

For roasted root chutney, slice 1 kg (2 lb) peeled parsnips and sweet potato, then roast with the shallots and red peppers. Continue as above, adding 1 teaspoon turmeric and 1 teaspoon smoked paprika instead of the allspice berries.

152

chilli & garlic chutney

Makes **2 jars**
Preparation time **15 minutes**
Cooking time **30 minutes**

500 g (1 lb) **fresh finger
  chillies**, red or green
6 **garlic cloves**, crushed
4 tablespoons **ground cumin**
2 tablespoons **ground
  turmeric**
1 large **onion**, finely chopped
1 tablespoon **salt**
25 g (1 oz) **root ginger**, grated
300 ml (½ pint) **groundnut oil**
3 tablespoons **muscovado
  sugar**
300 ml (½ pint) **white wine
  vinegar**

Remove the stalks from the chillies, then finely chop the chillies, seeds and all.

Add the chillies, garlic, cumin, turmeric, onion, salt, ginger and oil to a large saucepan and fry for 15 minutes, stirring frequently. Add the sugar and vinegar and bring to the boil. Reduce the heat to medium and simmer, covered, for 10 minutes, stirring from time to time.

Ladle into warm, dry jars. Disperse any air pockets with a skewer or small knife and cover with screw-top lids. Label and leave to mature in a cool, dark place for at least 3 weeks. Stir the chutney well before using as the oil will separate out on standing.

To serve, partner this chutney with curry.

For hot chilli & tamarind chutney, make as above, reducing the cumin to 2 tablespoons and adding 1 tablespoon tamarind paste and the grated rind and juice of 1 lime.

chestnut, onion & fennel chutney

Makes about **2 small jars**
Preparation time **15 minutes**
Cooking time **1 hour**
  25 minutes–1 hour
  30 minutes

60 ml (2½ fl oz) **olive oil**
4 large **red onions**, thinly
  sliced
1 **fennel bulb**, trimmed and
  thinly sliced
250 g (8 oz) **cooked, peeled
  chestnuts**, halved
100 g (3½ oz) **soft light
  brown sugar**
125 ml (4 fl oz) **cider vinegar**
125 ml (4 fl oz) **sweet sherry**
  or **marsala wine**
pepper

Heat the oil in a large saucepan, add the onions and fennel and cook over a gently heat for 25–30 minutes until the onions are very soft.

Add the chestnuts, sugar, vinegar and sherry or marsala to the pan, season well with pepper and stir. Simmer gently, uncovered, for about 1 hour, stirring from time to time, until the chutney has thickened.

Ladle into warm, dry jars. Disperse any air pockets with a skewer or small knife and cover with screw-top lids. Label and leave to mature in a cool, dark place for at least 3 weeks.

To serve, this chutney goes well with rustic bread topped with blue cheese.

For red onion & raisin chutney, fry 1.5 kg (3 lb) sliced red onions in 3 tablespoons olive oil for 10 minutes. Stir in 25 g (1 oz) light muscovado sugar, fry gently for 15 minutes until browned, then stir in an extra 200 g (7 oz) light muscovado sugar, 300 ml (½ pint) red wine vinegar, 200 g (7 oz) raisins, 3 chopped garlic cloves, 3 bay leaves, 1 tablespoon wholegrain mustard, salt and pepper. Simmer gently for 30 minutes, until thick, then pot as above.

peach & date chutney

Makes **3–4 jars**
Preparation time **10 minutes**
Cooking time **50 minutes**

12 **peaches**
500 g (1 lb) **onions**, finely
   chopped
2 **garlic cloves**, crushed
2 tablespoons **grated root**
   ginger
125 g (4 oz) **pitted dates**,
   chopped
250 g (8 oz) **demerara sugar**
300 ml (½ pint) **red wine**
   vinegar
salt and **pepper**

Place the peaches in a large bowl, cover with boiling water and leave to stand for about 1 minute, then drain and peel. Halve and stone the fruit and cut into thick slices.

Add the onions to a pan with the peaches, garlic, ginger, dates, sugar and vinegar. Add a generous sprinkling of salt and pepper and bring to the boil, stirring continuously, until the sugar has completely dissolved.

Reduce the heat and simmer, covered, stirring frequently, for 45 minutes, until the chutney has thickened.

Ladle into warm, dry jars. Disperse any air pockets with a skewer or small knife and cover with screw-top lids. Label and leave to mature in a cool, dark place for at least 3 weeks.

For peach & orange chutney, finely chop 1 whole orange and add this to a preserving pan with the onions, peaches, ginger, sugar and seasoning, as above, then add 125 g (4 oz) coarsely grated carrot and 300 ml (½ pint) white wine vinegar.

carrot & coriander chutney

Makes **4 jars**
Preparation time **25 minutes**
Cooking time **1–1¼ hours**

1 kg (2 lb) **carrots**, coarsely
  grated
1 **onion**, chopped
1 large **cooking apple**,
  quartered, cored, peeled
  and diced
4 cm (1½ inch) piece **root
  ginger**, peeled and finely
  chopped
4 **garlic cloves**, finely chopped
125 g (4 oz) **sultanas**
1 litre (1¾ pints) **distilled
  malt vinegar**
250 g (8 oz) **granulated
  sugar**
2 teaspoons **curry powder**
2 teaspoons **black mustard
  seeds** (optional)
½ teaspoon **salt**
pepper
small bunch of **coriander**,
  roughly chopped

Add all the ingredients except the coriander to
a preserving pan. Bring to the boil, then simmer,
uncovered, for 1–1¼ hours, stirring from time to time,
until the chutney is thick.

Remove from the heat and stir in the coriander.

Ladle into warm, dry jars, filling to the very top and
pressing down well. Disperse any air pockets with a
skewer or small knife and cover with screw-top lids.
Label and leave to mature in a cool, dark place for at
least 3 weeks.

For gingered parsnip & coriander chutney, omit the
carrots and add 1 kg (2 lb) peeled and grated parsnips,
using 1 teaspoon dried crushed red chillies instead of
the mustard seeds. Continue as above.

sweet potato & orange chutney

Makes **5 jars**
Preparation time **30 minutes**
Cooking time **1¾–2 hours**

750 g (1½ lb) **sweet
potatoes**, peeled and diced
500 g (1 lb) **onions**, chopped
250 g (8 oz) **sultanas**
250 g (8 oz) **carrots**, coarsely
grated
2 **oranges**, finely chopped,
including pith and peel
4 **garlic cloves**, finely chopped
45 g sachet **tamarind pulp**
300 g (10 oz) **light
muscovado sugar**
750 ml (1¼ pints) **distilled
malt vinegar**
1½ teaspoons **dried crushed
chillies**
1 teaspoon **salt**
1 teaspoon **black pepper**,
roughly crushed

Add all the ingredients to a preserving pan, cover and
cook gently for 1 hour, stirring from time to time. Remove
the lid and cook for ¾–1 hour, stirring more frequently
towards the end of cooking as the chutney thickens.

Ladle into warm, dry jars, filling to the very top and
pressing down well. Disperse any air pockets with a
skewer or small knife and cover with screw-top lids.
Label and leave to mature in a cool, dark place for at
least 3 weeks.

To serve, this chutney will enhance any cheeseboard.

For sweet potato, ginger & orange chutney, omit the
tamarind and add a 5 cm (2 inch) piece of peeled, finely
chopped root ginger.

andrew's plums

Makes **2 jars**
Preparation time **25 minutes**
Cooking time **1 hour**

½ teaspoon **cumin seeds**
½ teaspoon **fennel seeds**
1 teaspoon **coriander seeds**
½ teaspoon **dried chilli flakes**
1 kg (2 lb) **plums**, halved,
   stoned and diced
1 **onion**, chopped
2.5 cm (1 inch) piece **root
   ginger**, peeled and finely
   chopped
150 ml (¼ pint) **malt vinegar**
125 g (4 oz) **granulated
   sugar**
2 tablespoons **raisins**
juice of 1 **lemon**
salt and **pepper**

Crush the seeds roughly in a pestle and mortar, then toast in a hot preserving pan with the chilli flakes for a few seconds. Add all the remaining ingredients, then cover and simmer gently for 30 minutes, stirring from time to time.

Uncover the chutney and cook for 30 minutes, stirring until thick and pulpy. Mash with a potato masher, or blitz in a food processor or liquidizer, until smooth.

Ladle into warm, dry jars, filling to the very top and pressing down well. Disperse any air pockets with a skewer or small knife and cover with screw-top lids. Label and leave to mature in a cool, dark place for at least 3 weeks.

To serve, try adding to a cheese and salad sandwich.

For smooth plum & tomato chutney, add 500 g (1 lb) plums, stoned and diced, and 500 g (1 lb) roughly chopped tomatoes, then continue as above.

relishes

chillied red tomato relish

Makes **3 jars**
Preparation time **25 minutes**
Cooking time **1 hour**
  5 minutes

2 tablespoons **sunflower oil**
500 g (1 lb) **onions**, finely
  chopped
1 kg (2 lb) **tomatoes**, skinned
  (optional) and roughly
  chopped
4 **red finger chillies**,
  deseeded and chopped
3 stems **fresh thyme**
2 tablespoons **tomato purée**
1 teaspoon **smoked paprika**
300 ml (½ pint) **distilled
  malt vinegar**
250 g (8 oz) **granulated
  sugar**
salt and **pepper**

Heat the oil in a preserving pan, add the onions and fry for 5 minutes, until softened. Stir in the tomatoes and chillies, then add the remaining ingredients.

Cook, uncovered, for 1 hour, stirring more frequently towards the end of cooking as the relish thickens.

Ladle into warm, dry jars, pressing down well and filling the jars to the top. Disperse any air pockets with a skewer or small knife and cover with screw-top lids. Label and leave to mature in a cool, dark place for at least 3 weeks.

To serve, this relish goes well with Chinese-style pancake rolls, prawn sesame toast and tiny dumplings.

For jerked tomato relish, crush 1 teaspoon allspice berries and 1 teaspoon black peppercorns and add to the ingredients above along with ½ teaspoon ground cinnamon, 2 cloves garlic, finely chopped, and the grated rind and juice of 1 lime.

gooseberry relish with cardamom

Makes **2 jars**
Preparation time **25 minutes**
Cooking time **45 minutes**

1 kg (2 lb) **gooseberries**,
   topped and tailed
2 **onions**, chopped
10 **cardamom pods**, crushed
300 ml (½ pint) **distilled**
   malt vinegar
250 g (8 oz) **granulated**
   sugar
1 teaspoon **salt**
pepper

Add all the ingredients to a preserving pan.

Cook gently, uncovered, for 45 minutes until the gooseberries are soft, stirring from time to time, but more frequently towards the end of cooking as the relish thickens.

Ladle into warm, dry jars, pressing down well and filling the jars to the tops. Disperse any air pockets with a skewer or small knife and cover with screw-top lids. Label and leave to mature in a cool, dark place for at least 3 weeks.

To serve, this relish is very tasty with pork pie, little gem lettuce leaves and spring onions.

For spiced peach relish, omit the gooseberries and add 1 kg (2 lb) stoned and finely diced peaches. Cook with the onion, cardamom pods, a 5 cm (2 inch) cinnamon stick and 4 cloves as above.

sweet chilli & kaffir lime relish

Makes **2 assorted jars**
Preparation time **25 minutes**
Cooking time **1 hour**

500 g (1 lb) **onions**,
   finely chopped
4 **limes**, finely chopped
   including pith and peel
6 **green finger chillies**,
   including seeds, chopped
2 **green peppers**, cored,
   deseeded and diced
1 tablespoon **black mustard
   seeds**
1 teaspoon **turmeric**
4 **kaffir lime leaves**
300 ml (½ pint) **distilled
   malt vinegar**
500 g (1 lb) **granulated sugar**
1 teaspoon **salt**
pepper

Add all the ingredients to a preserving pan, cover and simmer gently for 45 minutes, stirring from time to time.

Remove the lid and cook for a further 15 minutes until the limes are soft, stirring more frequently towards the end of cooking as the relish thickens.

Ladle into warm, dry jars, pressing down well and filling the jars to the tops. Disperse any air pockets with a skewer or small knife and cover with screw-top lids. Label and leave to mature in a cool, dark place for at least 3 weeks.

For South Seas relish, add 250 g (8 oz) finely chopped onions, 250 g (8 oz) finely chopped fresh pineapple, 4 limes (including the pith and peel), chopped, 6 green finger chillies, finely chopped, 1 red and 1 green pepper, cored, deseeded and finely chopped, to a preserving pan with 1 teaspoon turmeric, 1 teaspoon allspice berries, roughly crushed, plus the vinegar, sugar, salt and pepper as above. Continue as above.

all-american tomato relish

Makes **2 jars**
Preparation time **20 minutes**
Cooking time **1 hour**
  5 minutes

2 tablespoons **sunflower oil**
2 **onions**, roughly chopped
2 **Granny Smith** or other sharp
  dessert apples, quartered,
  cored, peeled and diced
1 kg (2 lb) **tomatoes**, skinned
  (optional) and roughly
  chopped
300 ml (½ pint) **distilled**
  malt vinegar
250 g (8 oz) **granulated**
  sugar
2 tablespoons **tomato purée**
1 tablespoon **Worcestershire**
  sauce
1 teaspoon **paprika**
2 **bay leaves**
salt and **pepper**

Heat the oil in a saucepan, add the onions and fry for 5 minutes until softened. Add the apples and tomatoes, then stir in the remaining ingredients.

Cook over and gentle heat, uncovered, for 1 hour, stirring more frequently towards the end of cooking as the relish thickens.

Ladle into warm, dry jars, pressing down well and filling the jars to the top. Disperse any air pockets with a skewer or small knife and cover with screw-top lids. Label and leave to mature in a cool, dark place for at least 3 weeks.

To serve, this relish is perfect for dipping chunky chips.

For garlicky tomato relish, add 4 finely chopped garlic cloves to the preserving pan and cook as above.

174

cucumber & pepper relish

Makes **6 small jars**
Preparation time **30 minutes,
plus soaking**
Cooking time **25 minutes**

2 **cucumbers**, diced
50 g (2 oz) **salt**
1 tablespoon **sunflower oil**
2 **onions**, chopped
2 **red peppers**, cored,
deseeded and diced
300 ml (½ pint) **distilled
malt vinegar**
300 g (10 oz) **granulated
sugar**
1 teaspoon **dried crushed
red chillies**
½ teaspoon **turmeric**
2 teaspoons **mustard powder**
2 tablespoons **cornflour**
2 tablespoons **water**
½ teaspoon **peppercorns**,
roughly crushed

Layer the cucumbers in a bowl with the salt, cover with a plate, weight down and leave to soak for 4 hours. Tip into a colander, drain off the liquid, then rinse with cold water and drain well.

Heat the oil in a preserving pan, add the onions and fry for 5 minutes, stirring until softened. Add the red peppers and fry for a further 5 minutes.

Add the vinegar and sugar to the pan. Mix the chillies, turmeric, mustard powder and cornflour in a bowl, then stir in the measurement water and mix until smooth. Stir into the vinegar mixture and mix until smooth. Cook gently for 10 minutes, stirring from time to time, until thickened. Stir in the cucumber and peppercorns and cook for 5 minutes.

Ladle into warm, dry jars, pressing down well and making sure that the vinegar mixture covers the vegetables. Disperse any air pockets with a skewer or small knife and cover with screw-top lids. Label and leave to mature in a cool, dark place for at least 3 weeks.

For mixed pepper relish, halve 2 red, 2 green and 2 orange peppers, remove the seeds and core, then finely chop. Fry 1 chopped onion in 1 tablespoon sunflower oil until softened. Add the chopped peppers then fry for 5 minutes more. Add the vinegar and sugar, then mix the spices with cornflour and finish as above.

beetroot & apple relish

Makes **3 jars**
Preparation time **15 minutes**
Cooking time about **1½ hours**

500 g (1 lb) **cooking apples**,
    peeled, halved and cored
500 g (1 lb) **raw beetroot**,
    peeled
375 g (12 oz) **onions**, finely
    chopped
1 tablespoon finely chopped
    root ginger
2 large **garlic cloves**, crushed
1 teaspoon **paprika**
1 teaspoon **ground turmeric**
1 **cinnamon stick**
250 g (8 oz) **soft dark brown
    sugar**
450 ml (¾ pint) **red wine
    vinegar**

Grate the apples and beetroot into a large saucepan, then add all the remaining ingredients.

Bring to the boil, then reduce the heat and simmer, covered, stirring occasionally, for about 1½ hours, until the relish has thickened and the beetroot is tender.

Ladle into warm, dry jars. Disperse any air pockets with a skewer or small knife and cover with screw-top lids. Label and leave to mature in a cool, dark place for about 1 week.

To serve, partner this relish with pork chops.

For beetroot & horseradish relish, omit the turmeric and cinnamon and stir in a 5 cm (2 inch) raw horseradish root, peeled and grated. Continue as above.

sweetcorn relish

Makes **3 jars**
Preparation time **15 minutes**
Cooking time **25 minutes**

4 tablespoons **corn oil**
2 large **onions**, finely chopped
1 **green pepper**, cored,
  deseeded and finely
  chopped
1 **red pepper**, cored,
  deseeded and finely
  chopped
4 **celery sticks**, finely chopped
1 teaspoon **salt**
1 large **garlic clove**, crushed
2 **carrots**, peeled and cut into
  small cubes
50 g (2 oz) **sugar**
2 teaspoons **mustard powder**
750 g (1 ½ lb) **frozen
  sweetcorn**
450 ml (¾ pint) **vinegar**

Heat the oil in a large saucepan and add the onions, peppers and celery. Fry gently for 10 minutes until soft but not browned, then add the salt and garlic.

Add all the remaining ingredients and bring to the boil. Reduce the heat and cook, uncovered, for 15 minutes, stirring occasionally.

Ladle into warm, dry jars, pressing the vegetables well down into the juices, then top with screw-top lids and leave to cool. This relish does not need time to mature but, if not immediately consumed, label unopened jars and store in a cool, dark place.

To serve, this relish makes a great accompaniment to homemade burgers.

For hot sweetcorn relish, add 1 teaspoon smoked paprika and 1 teaspoon dried crushed red chillies when stirring in the vinegar.

tomato & pepper relish

Makes **4 jars**
Preparation time **20 minutes**
Cooking time **about**
30 minutes

1 kg (2 lb) **ripe tomatoes**,
skinned and chopped
1 kg (2 lb) **red peppers**,
cored, deseeded and
finely chopped
500 g (1 lb) **onions**, finely
chopped
2 **red chillies**, deseeded and
finely chopped
450 ml (¾ pint) **red wine**
vinegar
175 g (6 oz) **soft light**
brown sugar
4 tablespoons **mustard seeds**
2 tablespoons **celery seeds**
1 tablespoon **paprika**
2 teaspoons **salt**
2 teaspoons **pepper**

Combine all the ingredients in a large saucepan.

Bring the mixture to the boil over a moderate heat,
then reduce the heat and simmer, uncovered, for about
30 minutes until most of the liquid has evaporated and
the relish has a thick, pulpy consistency. Stir frequently
as the relish thickens.

Ladle into warm, dry jars. Disperse any air pockets with
a skewer or small knife and cover with screw-top lids.
Label and leave to mature in a cool, dark place for at
least 3 weeks.

For tomato & aubergine relish, replace the
red pepper with 1 kg (2 lb) aubergines cut into very
small dice and 2 tablespoons tomato purée, then
continue as above.

pickles

pickled peaches

Makes **1 large jar**
Preparation time **25 minutes**
Cooking time **6–8 minutes**

300 ml (½ pint) **white malt vinegar**
500 g (1 lb) **granulated sugar**
1 teaspoon **whole cloves**
1 teaspoon **whole allspice berries**
7 cm (3 inch) piece **cinnamon stick**, halved
1 kg (2 lb) **small peaches**, halved and stoned

Pour the vinegar into a large saucepan, add the sugar and spices and heat gently until the sugar has dissolved.

Add the peach halves and cook very gently for 4–5 minutes until just tender but still firm. Lift out of the syrup with a slotted spoon and pack tightly into a warmed large jar.

Boil the syrup for 2–3 minutes to concentrate the flavours, then pour over the fruit, making sure that the fruit is completely covered and the jar filled to the very top. Top up with a little extra warm vinegar if needed. Add a small piece of crumpled greaseproof paper to stop the fruit from rising out of the vinegar in the jar. Screw or clip on the lid, label and leave to cool.

After a few hours, the peaches will begin to rise in the jar, but as they become saturated with the syrup they will sink once more; at this point they will be ready to eat.

To serve, these peaches go well with slices of ham.

For pickled peach dressing, whisk 2 tablespoons spiced syrup from the jar of peaches with 3 tablespoons olive oil and 2 tablespoons finely chopped parsley or chives, then toss with 100 g (3½ oz) ready-washed salad leaves.

preserved lemons

Makes **1 large jar**
Preparation time **10 minutes**

8 **unwaxed baby lemons**
1 teaspoon **coriander seeds**
1 small **cinnamon stick**,
   bruised
2 **bay leaves**
50 g (2 oz) **sea salt**
juice of 1 **lemon**

Sprinkle a little salt into the bottom of a large, wide-necked jar, then layer the lemons, spices, bay leaves and remaining salt in the jar.

Add any remaining salt, the lemon juice and enough boiling water to cover the lemons. Top with an airtight lid and leave in a warm place for at least 2 weeks before using, for the lemon skins to soften. A white film may appear on the jar or on the lemons – this is harmless and can be rinsed off.

For pickled lemons with chilli & garlic, tuck 4 dried chillies into the jar with 8 unpeeled cloves of garlic and the lemons, and continue as above.

lime pickle

Makes **1 jar**
Preparation time **10 minutes**
Cooking time **5 minutes**

10 **limes**, each cut into
  6 wedges
125 g (4 oz) **sea salt**
1 tablespoon **fenugreek
  seeds**
1 tablespoon **black mustard
  seeds**
1 tablespoon **chilli powder**
1 tablespoon **ground turmeric**
300 ml (½ pint) **vegetable oil**
½ teaspoon **ground
  asafoetida**

Put the limes into a large jar and cover with the salt.

Dry-fry the fenugreek and mustard seeds in a small nonstick frying pan, then grind them to a powder in either a mortar with a pestle, a spice grinder or a coffee grinder kept specially for the purpose.

Add the ground seeds, chilli powder and turmeric to the limes and mix well.

Heat the oil in a small frying pan until smoking, add the asafoetida and fry for 30 seconds. Pour the oil over the limes and mix well.

Cover the jar with a clean cloth and leave to mature for 10 days in a bright, warm place. Top with an airtight lid. Label and store in a cool, dark place.

For pickled kumquats, halve 30 kumquats and pack into a jar with the salt as above. Dry-fry 1 tablespoon coriander seeds with 2 teaspoons cumin seeds, coarsely grind in a pestle and mortar, mix with 1 teaspoon dried chilli seeds, 1 teaspoon turmeric and 1 teaspoon smoked paprika, then stir in 300 ml (½ pint) vegetable oil and pour over the kumquats. Continue as above.

sweet pickled cucumbers

Makes **3 jars**
Preparation time **25 minutes,
  plus soaking**
Cooking time **5–6 minutes**

2 large **cucumbers**, thinly
  sliced
1 medium **onion**, thinly sliced
50 g (2 oz) **salt**
450 ml (¾ pint) **white wine
  vinegar**
375 g (12 oz) **granulated
  sugar**
½ teaspoon **turmeric**
2 teaspoons **fennel seeds**
½ teaspoon **dried crushed
  red chillies**
¼ teaspoon **peppercorns**,
  roughly crushed

Layer the cucumbers, onions and salt in a bowl, cover with a plate and weight down, then leave to soak for 4 hours.

Meanwhile, pour the vinegar into a saucepan, add the sugar and the remaining ingredients and heat gently, stirring from time to time, until the sugar has dissolved, then leave to cool.

Tip the cucumber and onions into a colander and drain off the liquid. Rinse with plenty of cold water and drain well.

Reheat the vinegar mixture until just boiling, add the drained cucumber and onion, cook for 1 minute, then lift out of the vinegar with a draining spoon and pack into warm, dry jars. Boil the remaining vinegar mixture for 4–5 minutes until syrupy, then leave to cool.

Pour the cold vinegar mixture over the cucumber slices to completely cover and to fill the jars to the top (adding a little extra vinegar if needed). Screw on lids, label and leave to mature in a cool, dark place for 3–4 weeks.

For sweet pickled oranges, thinly slice 6 thin-skinned oranges, put into a saucepan, cover with water and bring to the boil. Simmer for 45 minutes until the slices are tender. Drain. Make up the vinegar mixture as above, add the cooked orange slices and simmer for 10 minutes or until the orange rind becomes transparent. Lift out the oranges with a slotted spoon and pack into warm, dry jars. Boil the syrup and finish as above.

spiced pickled beetroot

Makes **3 jars**
Preparation time **25 minutes**
Cooking time **33–63 minutes**

1 kg (2 lb) **beetroot** (about 10),
    leaves trimmed to about 2 cm
    (¾ in) from the tops
600 ml (1 pint) **malt vinegar**
125 g (4 oz) **granulated
    sugar**
3.5 cm (1½ inch) piece of
    root ginger, peeled and
    finely chopped
4 teaspoons **allspice berries**,
    roughly crushed
½ teaspoon **black
    peppercorns**, roughly
    crushed
½ teaspoon **salt**

Cook the beetroot in a saucepan of boiling water for 30–60 minutes, depending on their size, or until a knife can be inserted into the largest one easily. Drain, leave to cool, then peel off the skins with a small knife.

Meanwhile, pour the vinegar into a saucepan, add the sugar and remaining ingredients. Heat gently, stirring from time to time, until the sugar has dissolved. Increase the heat and simmer for 3 minutes, then remove from the heat and leave to cool.

Cut the beetroot into chunks and pack into warm, dry jars. Pour over the cold vinegar mixture to cover the beetroot completely and so that the vinegar comes to the top of the jars (adding a little extra vinegar if needed). Screw on lids, label and leave to mature in a cool, dark place for 3–4 weeks.

To serve, try tossing some mixed lettuce leaves in a crème fraîche dressing, then top with flakes of peppered smoked mackerel and spoonfuls of drained beetroot with just a little of the vinegar mixture.

For chilli spiced beetroot, omit the ginger from the spiced vinegar mixture and add 1 teaspoon dried crushed red chilli flakes and 3 star anise instead. Continue as above.

pickled shallots

Makes **1 very large jar**
Preparation time **30 minutes,
 plus soaking and standing**
Cooking time **5 minutes**

625 g (1¼ lb) **small shallots**
40 g (1½ oz) **salt**
450 ml (¾ pint) **sherry
 vinegar**
125 g (4 oz) **caster sugar**
125 g (4 oz) **light muscovado
 sugar**
2 **garlic cloves**, unpeeled
4 small **bay leaves**
4 sprigs **thyme**
4 sprigs **rosemary**
pinch of salt
½ teaspoon **peppercorns**,
 roughly crushed

Trim a little off the tops and roots of the shallots, then put into a bowl and cover with boiling water. Leave to soak for 3 minutes, then pour off the water and re-cover with cold water. Lift the shallots out one at a time and peel off the brown skins. Drain and layer in a bowl with the salt. Leave overnight.

Tip the shallots into a colander and drain off as much liquid as possible. Rinse with cold water, drain and dry with kitchen towel.

Add the vinegar and sugar to a saucepan with the garlic cloves, half the herbs, a pinch of salt and peppercorns. Heat gently until the sugar dissolves, stirring from time to time. Increase the heat to medium and simmer for 5 minutes. Leave to cool.

Pack the shallots tightly into warm, dry jars with the remaining herbs. Strain and pour the cold vinegar syrup over the shallots, making sure that the shallots are covered with the vinegar to the very top. Cover with screw-top lids. Label and leave to mature in a cool, dark place for 3–4 weeks.

For chillied pickled shallots, omit the thyme and rosemary and add 1½ teaspoons dried crushed chillies instead. Continue as above.

torshi

Makes **3 assorted jars**
Preparation time **30 minutes,
 plus soaking and standing**
Cooking time **2 minutes**

200 g (7 oz) **courgettes**,
 sliced
200 g (7 oz) **carrots**, sliced
150 g (5 oz) **French beans**,
 halved
1 **fennel bulb**, sliced
1 **cauliflower**, cut into small
 florets
250 g (8 oz) **small pickling
 onions**, peeled
100 g (3½ oz) **salt**
1.14 litre bottle **distilled malt
 vinegar** or **white wine
 vinegar**
250 g (8 oz) **granulated
 sugar**
2 teaspoons **caraway seeds**
2 teaspoons **coriander seeds**,
 roughly crushed
½ teaspoon **peppercorns**,
 roughly crushed
6 small **dried red chillies**
6 **garlic cloves**, peeled and
 halved
4 stems **dill** or **fennel**

Layer the vegetables in a bowl with the salt, cover with a plate and weight down, then leave to soak overnight.

Pour the vinegar into a saucepan and add the sugar, caraway seeds, coriander seeds and peppercorns, then the dried chillies, garlic and 3 stems of dill or fennel. Bring to the boil, stirring until the sugar has dissolved, then set aside for the flavours to mingle.

Next day, drain off the liquid from the vegetables, rinse with cold water, drain well, then pat dry with kitchen paper. Pack into warm, dry jars with the halved garlic and chillies from the vinegar mixture and the remaining fresh dill or fennel. Discard the cooked herbs from the spiced vinegar, then pour the cold vinegar mixture into the jars to the very top of the jars, making sure that the vegetables are completely covered (there is no need to strain the vinegar first).

Secure the lids, label and leave to mature in a cool, dark place for 3–4 weeks.

For pickled red cabbage, add 1 finely shredded medium red cabbage in place of the carrot, cauliflower, beans and onions, then salt and leave overnight as above. Drain off the liquid, then pack into warm, dry jars and pour over the cold flavoured vinegar as above.

three-bean mustard pickle

Makes **4 jars**
Preparation time **25 minutes**
Cooking time **23 minutes**

250 g (8 oz) **podded
   broad beans**
250 g (8 oz) **French beans**,
   each cut into three
250 g (8 oz) **runner beans**,
   thinly sliced
500 ml bottle **cider** or **white
   wine vinegar**
375 g (12 oz) **caster sugar**
2 **medium onions**, chopped
3 **garlic cloves**, finely
   chopped
2 tablespoons **cornflour**
1 tablespoon **turmeric**
1 tablespoon **mustard
   powder**
1 tablespoon **whole grain
   mustard**
2 teaspoons **fennel seeds**,
   roughly crushed
1 teaspoon **salt**
pepper
2 tablespoons **water**

Bring a large saucepan of water to the boil, add the beans, cover and bring back to the boil, then cook for 3 minutes. Drain and refresh with cold water, then drain again.

Pour the vinegar and sugar into a preserving pan, add the onions and garlic, then cover and bring to the boil. Reduce the heat and simmer for 10 minutes.

Mix the remaining dry ingredients together in a bowl, then mix to a smooth paste with the measurement water. Stir into the vinegar mixture and cook, uncovered, for 5 minutes, stirring until thickened slightly.

Add the blanched vegetables, cook for a further 5 minutes, stirring, until the vegetables are just tender, then ladle into warm, dry jars, pressing the vegetables down below the liquid with a fork and making sure there are no air pockets. Label and leave to mature in a cool, dark place for 3–4 weeks.

For curried bean pickle, use distilled malt vinegar instead of the wine or cider vinegar, and add 2 tablespoons mild curry powder in place of the mustard powder and wholegrain mustard. Continue as above.

piccalilli

Makes **2–3 jars**
Preparation time **10 minutes,
plus standing**
Cooking time **25 minutes**

1 small **cauliflower**, broken
into small florets, large stalks
discarded
½ **cucumber**, peeled and
roughly chopped
2 **onions**, chopped
2 large **carrots**, peeled and
cut into chunks
about 50 g (2 oz) **salt**
2 tablespoons **plain flour**
300 ml (½ pint) **cider vinegar**
250 g (8 oz) **granulated
sugar**
½ teaspoon **ground turmeric**
½ teaspoon **ground ginger**
2 teaspoons **mustard powder**
pepper

Layer the vegetables in a large bowl, sprinkling each
layer with salt, then cover and leave to stand overnight.
The next day, lightly rinse and thoroughly dry them.

Mix the flour to a smooth paste with a little of the
vinegar. Heat the remaining vinegar in a large saucepan
with the sugar, spices and mustard powder over a low
heat, stirring continuously, until the sugar has dissolved.
Increase the heat and bring to the boil, then season the
mixture generously with pepper and add the vegetables.
Bring back to the boil, then reduce the heat and
simmer, uncovered, for 10 minutes.

Remove the pan from the heat and gradually stir in the
flour mixture. Return to the heat, bring to the boil and
simmer for a further 5 minutes.

Ladle into warm, dry jars. Disperse any air pockets with
a skewer or small knife and cover with screw-top lids.
Label and leave to mature in a cool, dark place for at
least 3 weeks.

To serve, partner with slivers of Parma ham.

For Caribbean vegetable pickle, use 1 large
aubergine cut into cubes, ½ small butternut squash,
deseeded, peeled and cubed, ½ cauliflower, cut into
florets, and 100 g (3½ oz) green beans, cut into 2.5 cm
(1 inch) lengths. Mix with 1 chopped onion, then layer
with 50g (2 oz) salt, soak and continue as above.

honey pickled chillies

Makes **2 jars**
Preparation time **15 minutes**
Cooking time **7–8 minutes**

500 g (1 lb) whole **red finger chillies**
450 ml (¾ pint) **cider** or **white wine vinegar**
4 tablespoons **set honey**
4 tablespoons **light muscovado sugar**
4 **bay leaves**
4 **sprigs thyme**
4 **garlic cloves**, peeled and sliced
2.5 cm (1 inch) piece **root ginger**, peeled and finely chopped
1 teaspoon **coriander seeds**
1 teaspoon **salt**

Add the chillies to a saucepan of boiling water and cook for 2–3 minutes until just softened. Tip into a colander, rinse with cold water and drain well.

Pour the vinegar into the drained pan and add all the remaining ingredients. Heat gently until the sugar has dissolved, then cook over a medium heat for 5 minutes.

Pack the chillies and herbs from the vinegar tightly into 2 jars, then pour over the hot vinegar mixture, making sure that the chillies are completely covered by the vinegar. Cover with screw-top lids, label and leave to mature in a cool, dark place for 3–4 weeks.

For pickled baby peppers, omit the chillies and blanch 500 g (1 lb) mixed baby red, yellow and orange peppers in the same way as the chillies, then continue as above.

japanese pickled ginger

Makes **2 small jars**
Preparation time **15 minutes,
  plus standing**
Cooking time **3–4 minutes**

500 g (1 lb) **root ginger**,
  peeled and very thinly sliced
50 g (2 oz) **salt**
250 ml (8 fl oz) **rice vinegar**
100 g (3½ oz) **granulated
  sugar**
2 **Thai green** or **red chillies**,
  sliced
10 **white peppercorns**

Layer the ginger and salt in a bowl, cover with a plate, weight down and leave to stand overnight.

Tip the ginger into a colander and drain off as much liquid as possible. Rinse with cold water, drain and dry with kitchen towel.

Add the vinegar, sugar, chilli slices and peppercorns to a saucepan, heat gently until the sugar has dissolved, then bring to the boil and cook over a medium heat for 2–3 minutes. Add the ginger and cook for 1 minute.

Pack the ginger and hot syrup into warm, dry jars, pressing the ginger below the vinegar mixture so that it is completely covered and the jar filled to the very top. Cover with screw-top lids. Label and leave to mature in a cool, dark place for 3–4 weeks.

To serve, use as an accompaniment for sushi.

For pickled garlic, separate 4 garlic bulbs into cloves, then peel and cut each clove in half. Continue as above, omitting the ginger.

festive fruit
preserves

mincemeat

Makes **6 jars**
Preparation time **20–30**
  minutes, plus standing

500 g (1 lb) **currants**, chopped
500 g (1 lb) **sultanas**, chopped
500 g (1 lb) **seedless raisins**,
  chopped
500 g (1 lb) **chopped**
  mixed peel
125 g (4 oz) **blanched**
  almonds, finely chopped
500 g (1 lb) **cooking apples**,
  peeled, cored and coarsely
  grated
500 g (1 lb) **soft dark brown**
  sugar
250 g (8 oz) **shredded suet**
1 teaspoon **ground nutmeg**
  or **grated nutmeg**
1 teaspoon **ground cinnamon**
1 teaspoon **ground mixed**
  spice
grated rind of 2 **lemons**
juice of 1 **lemon**
2–4 tablespoons **brandy**

Put the currants, sultanas, raisins, peel and almonds into a large bowl. Add the apples, sugar, suet, spices and lemon rind and juice and stir to mix thoroughly. Cover the bowl with clingfilm and leave the mincemeat to stand for 2 days.

Stir the mincemeat very thoroughly, then add the brandy.

Pack the mincemeat into warm, dry jars. Cover with waxed discs. Cover with screw-top lids, or with waxed discs and cellophane tops secured with elastic bands. Label and store in a cool, dry place for at least 2 weeks before using.

For cranberry mincemeat, use 400 g (13 oz) each of currants, sultanas and seedless raisins and 300 g (10 oz) dried cranberries. Continue as above.

apricot & ginger mincemeat

Makes **4 jars**
Preparation time **30 minutes,
plus standing**

50 g (2 oz) **crystallized
ginger**, finely chopped
250 g (8 oz) ready-to-eat **dried
apricots**, finely chopped
250 g (8 oz) **raisins**, finely
chopped
175 g (6 oz) **sultanas**, finely
chopped
175 g (6 oz) **currants**
50 g (2 oz) **chopped mixed
peel**
50 g (2 oz) **blanched
almonds**, chopped
250 g (8 oz) **cooking apples**,
peeled, cored and grated
juice and grated rind of
3 oranges
juice and grated rind of
2 lemons
250 g (8 oz) **soft light brown
sugar**
375 g (12 oz) **carrots**, peeled
and grated
¼ teaspoon **grated nutmeg**
½ teaspoon **ground mixed
spice**
150 ml (¼ pint) **brandy**
4 tablespoons **rum**

Put the ginger, apricots, raisins and sultanas into a
large bowl with the currants, mixed peel and almonds.

Put the apples into a separate bowl and mix in the
orange and lemon rinds and juices, then stir into the
chopped fruit with the sugar.

Add the carrots to the bowl with the spices, brandy and
rum, then cover the bowl with clingfilm and leave the
mincemeat to stand for 2 days, stirring frequently.

Pack the mincemeat into warm, dry jars. Cover with
screw-top lids, or with waxed discs and cellophane tops
secured with elastic bands. Label and store in a cool,
dark place to mature for 3–4 weeks before using.

To serve, use as a filling for mince pies.

For mulled wine cherry mincemeat, mix 125 g
(4 oz) dried cherries with 125 g (4 oz) chopped ready-
to-eat dried apricots, then add to the dried vine fruits,
peel, almonds, apples, citrus rinds and juice and spices
as above. Stir in 150 ml (¼ pint) port and 4 tablespoons
brandy and continue as above.

cranberry mincemeat with port

Makes **4 assorted jars**

Preparation time **20 minutes, plus standing**

Cooking time **5 minutes**

250 g (8 oz) **cranberries**

1 large **cooking apple** (about 375 g/12 oz), peeled, cored and diced

3 tablespoons **water**

500 g (1 lb) bag **luxury mixed dried fruit**

1 teaspoon **ground cinnamon**

½ teaspoon **freshly grated nutmeg**

¼ teaspoon **ground cloves**

200 g (7 oz) **soft light brown sugar**

125 g (4 oz) **shredded vegetable suet**

grated rind of 1 **orange**

125 ml (4 fl oz) **ruby port**

Put the cranberries and apple into a saucepan with the measurement water and cook, uncovered, for 5 minutes, stirring occasionally, until the fruits are softened but still holding their shape. Leave to cool in the pan.

Put the dried fruit into a large bowl and mix in the remaining ingredients. Stir in the cooked fruit, then cover the bowl with clingfilm and leave to stand overnight.

Stir the mincemeat mixture, then pack into warm, dry jars. Cover with screw-top lids, or with waxed discs and cellophane tops secured with elastic bands. Label and store in a cool, dark place to mature for 3–4 weeks before using.

To serve, use as a filling for mince pies.

For prune & whisky mincemeat, add 250 g (8 oz) stoned and diced ready-to-eat prunes to a pan with the apple and water as above. Add the dried fruits and continue adding the spices, sugar, suet, orange rind and 125 ml (4 fl oz) whisky.

figs in vanilla syrup

Makes **1 jar**
Preparation time **20 minutes**
Cooking time **about**
  45 minutes

8–9 firm **fresh figs**, halved
100 g (4 oz) **caster sugar**
200 ml (7 fl oz) **water**
½ **vanilla pod**, slit lengthways
½ teaspoon **citric acid**

Pack the figs into a warm, dry jar with the cut sides facing out. Pack the centre of the jar tightly and put two halves, cut side uppermost, in the top of the jar.

Put the sugar, measurement water and vanilla pod into a saucepan. Slowly bring to the boil and heat, stirring continuously, until the sugar has completely dissolved. Boil for 1 minute, then remove from the heat.

Lift the vanilla pod out of the syrup and, using a small knife, scrape out the black seeds into the syrup and stir in the citric acid. Tuck the vanilla pod down the side of the jar.

Pour the syrup over the figs to cover completely and come almost to the brim of the jar. Top up with boiling water if needed and seal the jar. Stand the jar on a baking sheet lined with several sheets of folded newspaper and bake in a preheated oven, 150°C (300°F), Gas Mark 2, for 40 minutes until the syrup has turned a delicate pink and the figs are just beginning to rise in the jar.

Using oven gloves, transfer the jar to a wooden board, secure the lid and leave to cool completely. When cold, check the jar seals, label and store in a cool, dark place.

For apricots in marsala syrup, halve 8–9 fresh apricots and pack tightly into a jar. Make the syrup as above with 125 g (4 oz) caster sugar and 250 ml (8 fl oz) water. Take off the heat and stir in 150 ml (¼ pint) marsala wine and ½ teaspoon citric acid. Pour the syrup over the apricots and continue as above.

blueberries in kirsch

Makes **1 jar**
Preparation time **10 minutes,
    plus standing**

175 g (6 oz) **blueberries**,
    destalked
50 g (2 oz) **caster sugar**
100 ml (3½ fl oz) **kirsch**

Pick over the blueberries, discarding any very soft
ones. Prick each berry with a fork, then layer in a clean,
dry jar, sprinkling each layer with some sugar.

Pour over the kirsch. Seal tightly and shake once or twice.

Leave in a cool place and turn the jar upside down
every day for 4 days until the sugar has completely
dissolved. Label and leave to mature in a cool, dark
place for 3–4 weeks.

To serve, drizzle over pancakes served with vanilla
ice cream.

For cherries in brandy, omit the blueberries and use
175 g (6 oz) small firm cherries that have had their
stalks removed. Prick the cherries and layer in the jar
with the sugar, then top up with brandy in place of
kirsch. Continue as above.

herby pickled plums

Makes **3 jars**
Preparation time **20 minutes**
Cooking time **3 minutes**

750 ml (1 ¼ pints) **white wine vinegar**
500 g (1 lb) **caster sugar**
7 **rosemary sprigs**
7 **thyme sprigs**
7 **small bay leaves**
4 **lavender sprigs** (optional)
4 **garlic cloves**, unpeeled
1 teaspoon **salt**
½ teaspoon **multi-coloured peppercorns**
1.5 kg (3 lb) **firm red plums**, washed and pricked

Pour the vinegar and sugar into a saucepan, add 4 each of the rosemary and thyme sprigs and bay leaves, all the lavender, if using, the garlic, salt and peppercorns. Cook gently, stirring once or twice, until the sugar has dissolved. Bring to the boil, then boil for 3 minutes until the mixture becomes syrupy.

Pack the plums tightly into warm, dry jars and tuck the remaining fresh herbs into them. Strain in the hot vinegar, making sure that the plums are completely covered, then top with airtight lids.

Label and leave to mature in a cool, dark place for 3–4 weeks. The plums will lose colour slightly.

For pickled red peppers, cut the tops off 4 red peppers and scoop out the core and seeds. Add to a saucepan of boiling water and cook for 3 minutes until just softened. Drain well, then dry on kitchen towel. Heat 600 ml (1 pint) distilled malt vinegar with 250 g (8 oz) granulated sugar until the sugar has dissolved, then cover and simmer for 10 minutes. Pack the peppers in a jar, pour over the hot vinegar to cover, and screw on the lid.

orange & whisky marmalade

Makes **4 jars**
Preparation time **30 minutes**
Cooking time **1 hour
30 minutes–1 hour
35 minutes**

1 kg (2 lb) **Seville or bitter
oranges** (about 6)
juice of 1 **lemon**
1 kg (2 lb) **granulated sugar**,
warmed
4 tablespoons **whisky**

Add the whole oranges to a saucepan so that they fit snugly in a single layer. Just cover with cold water, then bring to the boil, cover with a lid and cook gently for 1 hour or until the oranges can be pierced easily with a small sharp knife or wooden cocktail stick. Leave to cool.

Lift the oranges out of the pan with a slotted spoon, draining well. Reserve 900 ml (1½ pints) of the cooking liquid and discard any extra. Halve the cooked oranges, scoop out the pips and reserve. Cut the oranges into thin slices. Add the orange slices to the preserving pan with the pips tied in a square of muslin, the measured cooking liquid and the lemon juice, then simmer over medium heat for 10 minutes until the orange slices are very tender.

Add the sugar and heat gently, stirring from time to time, until the sugar has dissolved. Bring to the boil, then boil rapidly until setting point is reached (20–25 minutes). Lift out the muslin bag, squeezing well. Stir in the whisky and leave to cool for 10 minutes.

Ladle into warm, dry jars, filling to the very top. Cover with screw-top lids, or with waxed discs and cellophane tops secured with elastic bands. Label and leave to cool.

For chunky orange marmalade, use the same weight of ordinary oranges and when measuring the water, add the juice of 2 lemons, then continue as above but omit the whisky.

ginger marmalade

Makes **5 jars**
Preparation time **30 minutes,**
  plus standing
Cooking time **2¾ hours**

8 **lemons**
2 large **oranges**
2.5 litres (4 pints) **water**
125 g (4 oz) **root ginger,**
  sliced and finely shredded
1.5 kg (3 lb) **granulated**
  sugar, warmed
15 g (½ oz) **butter** (optional)

Pare the rind from the fruits with a vegetable peeler and cut into fine shreds. Halve the fruits and squeeze out the juice, then put the juice and rind into a large saucepan with the measurement water and ginger.

Chop the fruit halves, including the pith, and tie in a square of muslin. Add this to the pan and slowly bring the mixture to the boil. Reduce the heat, cover the pan and simmer for 2 hours or until the ginger and rind are completely tender. Take the pan off the heat and leave to stand until the muslin is cool enough to handle, then squeeze all the juices back into the marmalade and discard the muslin bag.

Add the sugar to the pan and cook over a low heat, stirring continuously, until the sugar has dissolved. Increase the heat and bring to the boil, then boil hard to setting point (20–30 minutes). Skim with a draining spoon or stir in butter if needed, then leave the marmalade to stand for 15 minutes to allow the fruit to settle.

Stir well, then ladle into warm, dry jars. Cover with clip- or screw-top lids, or with waxed discs and cellophane tops secured with elastic bands. Label and store in a cool, dark place.

For lime marmalade, cut 8 large limes into quarters lengthways and then into long, very fine slices, removing all the pips. Mix the fruit in a large saucepan. Add 1.5 litres (2½ pints) water, bring to the boil, then reduce the heat, cover and simmer for 1½ hours. Add 1.5 kg (3 lb) sugar and proceed as above.

winter fig & orange jam

Makes **6 jars**
Preparation time **20 minutes**
Cooking time **45–50 minutes**

500 g (1 lb) ready-to-eat
  dried figs
1.5 kg (3 lb) **cooking apples**
2 **oranges**
900 ml (1½ pints) **water**
2 teaspoons **ground
  cinnamon**
1.25 kg (2½ lb) **granulated
  sugar**, warmed

Chop the figs, then add to a preserving pan. Quarter, core and peel the apples, then cut into small dice. Finely chop the whole oranges or roughly chop, then blitz in a food processor until finely chopped. Add to the preserving pan with the measurement water and cinnamon. Cover and cook gently for 30 minutes, stirring from time to time, until the fruit is very soft.

Add the sugar and heat gently, stirring occasionally, until the sugar has dissolved. Bring to the boil, then boil rapidly for 15–20 minutes until very thick. This jam has more of a chutney-like consistency, so stir more frequently the thicker it becomes so that it doesn't catch on the base of the preserving pan.

Ladle into warm, dry jars, filling to the very top. Cover with screw-top lids, or with waxed discs and cellophane tops secured with elastic bands. Label and leave to cool.

For winter apricot & orange jam, use 500 g (1 lb) diced ready-to-eat dried apricots instead of the figs. Continue as above.

apricot & cointreau curd

Makes **2 jars**
Preparation time **25 minutes**
Cooking time **55 minutes–**
  1 hour 5 minutes

125 g (4 oz) **ready-to-eat**
  dried apricots, diced
150 ml (¼ pint) **water**
juice of 2 **lemons**
125 g (4 oz) **butter**, diced
375 g (12 oz) **caster sugar**
4 **eggs**, beaten
3 tablespoons **Cointreau**
  or **Grand Marnier**

Add the apricots and measurement water to a saucepan, then cover and cook gently for about 15 minutes until soft. Leave to cool for 10–15 minutes.

Purée the apricots in a food processor or liquidizer with the lemon juice. Melt the butter in a large bowl set over a saucepan of simmering water. Add the apricot purée and sugar, then strain in the eggs and mix together. Cook for 40–50 minutes, stirring from time to time until the sugar has dissolved and the mixture has thickened.

Stir in the liqueur, then ladle into warm, dry jars, filling to the very top. Cover with screw-top lids, or with waxed discs and cellophane tops secured with elastic bands. Label and leave to cool, then store in the refrigerator for up to 2 weeks.

To serve, this curd mingles perfectly with lightly whipped cream and crumbled meringues, for an easy pudding.

For apricot & orange curd, cook the apricots in 150 ml (¼ pint) orange juice from a chilled carton. Continue as above, but omit the liqueur.

blackcurrant & mulled wine jelly

Makes **4 jars**

Preparation time **30 minutes, plus straining**

Cooking time **55 minutes– 1 hour**

1.5 kg (3 lb) fresh or frozen **blackcurrants**

750 ml (1¼ pints) **water**

250 ml (8 fl oz) **red wine**

10 cm (4 inch) **piece cinnamon stick**, broken into pieces

1 teaspoon **whole cloves**

rind of **1 orange**

rind of **1 lemon**

about 1.25 kg (2¾ lb) **granulated sugar**

15 g (½ oz) **butter** (optional)

Add the blackcurrants, measurement water and wine to a preserving pan, then add the spices and fruit rinds. Bring to the boil, then cover and simmer gently for 40 minutes, stirring and mashing the fruit from time to time with a fork, until soft. Allow to cool slightly, then pour into a scalded jelly bag suspended over a large bowl and allow to drip for several hours.

Measure the clear liquid and then pour back into a preserving pan. Weigh 500 g (1 lb) sugar for every 600 ml (1 pint) of liquid, then pour into the pan. Heat gently, stirring from time to time, until the sugar has dissolved.

Bring to the boil, then boil rapidly until setting point is reached (15–20 minutes). Skim with a draining spoon or stir in butter if needed.

Ladle into warm, dry jars, filling to the very top. Cover with screw-top lids, or with waxed discs and cellophane tops secured with elastic bands. Label and leave to cool.

To serve, this jelly can be spooned on top of cup cakes that have been decorated with piped buttercream.

For cranberry mulled wine jelly, make up the jelly with 1.5 kg (3 lb) cranberries instead of the blackcurrants. Continue as above.

cranberry & red wine chutney

Makes **3 assorted jars**
Preparation time **30 minutes**
Cooking time **1¼–1½ hours**

500 g (1 lb) **fresh** or **frozen
cranberries** (if frozen, there
is no need to defrost first)
500 g (1 lb) **red onions**,
thinly sliced
250 g (8 oz) **mixed dried fruit**
250 g (8 oz) **light muscovado
sugar**
150 ml (¼ pint) **red wine**
150 ml (¼ pint) **red wine
vinegar**
2 teaspoons **ground mixed
spice**
1 teaspoon **dried crushed
chillies**
1 teaspoon **salt**
½ teaspoon **pepper**

Add all the ingredients to a preserving pan, cover and simmer gently for 1 hour, stirring from time to time, until softened.

Remove the lid and cook for 15–30 minutes until thick, stirring more frequently towards the end of cooking, until the cranberries are very soft and the chutney is thick.

Spoon into warm, dry jars, filling to the very top and pressing down well. Disperse any air pockets with a skewer or small knife. Cover with screw-top lids, label and leave to cool.

To serve, this chutney goes perfectly with cold sliced turkey, watercress and cherry tomatoes.

For Christmas plum chutney, omit the cranberries and add 500 g (1 lb) stoned and sliced plums instead, and 300 ml (½ pint) red wine vinegar instead of the vinegar and red wine. Continue as above.

index

acknowledgements

Executive Editor: Eleanor Maxfield
Senior Editor: Leanne Bryan
Executive Art Editor: Juliette Norsworthy
Designer: Penny Stock
Art Director: Isabel de Cordova
Photographer: Stephen Conroy
Home Economist: Sara Lewis
Props Stylist: Kim Sullivan
Production: Caroline Alberti

Special photography: Octopus Publishing Group/
Stephen Conroy
Other photography: Octopus Publishing Group/
Stephen Conroy 11, 12 left, 12 centre, 12 right, 13 left,
13 right, 14, 17, 35, 39, 45, 47, 75, 113, 121, 149, 155,
157, 159, 179, 181, 189, 191, 203, 213, 215, 217, 221;
/Lis Parsons 85, 183, 211, 219, 225.